D0992595

The Greenest Nation?

History for a Sustainable Future
Michael Egan, series editor

Derek Wall, *Culture, Conflict, and Ecology: The Commons in History*

Frank Uekötter, *The Greenest Nation? A New History of German Environmentalism*

The Greenest Nation?

A New History of German Environmentalism

Frank Uekötter

The MIT Press
Cambridge, Massachusetts
London, England

MIT Press books may be purchased at special quantity discounts for business or sales promotional use. For information, please email special_sales@ mitpress.mit.edu.

This book was set in Sabon by the MIT Press. Printed and bound in the United States of America.

Library of Congress Cataloging-in-Publication Data

Uekötter, Frank, 1970-
The greenest nation? : a new history of German environmentalism / Frank Uekötter.
  pages   cm.
Includes bibliographical references and index.
ISBN 978-0-262-02732-8 (hardcover : alk. paper)
1. Environmentalism–History—21st century. 2. Environmental policy–History–21st century. 3. Environmentalism–Germany–History–20th century.
4. Environmentalism--GE195.U45 2014
333.720943--dc23
2013032416

10   9   8   7   6   5   4   3   2   1

Contents

Foreword

Michael Egan

It is hardly hyperbole to assert that we live in a state of environmental crisis. Human-induced climate change is already threatening plant and animal biodiversity and human habitats. Globally there is an uneven distribution of environmental amenities and hazards. Our food and our bodies are increasingly burdened with a cocktail of toxic chemicals. Despite our advances in science, technology, and medicine, more rather than fewer children are diagnosed with asthma and leukemia. Human population growth is seriously challenging the planet's carrying capacity. And we are consuming more natural resources at an unsustainable rate. This environmental deterioration has a history that is ingrained in a human social, political, and technological past that we have yet to fully understand. The History for a Sustainable Future series seeks to shed light on this history as a means of better focusing contemporary debate.

It is a bit of a funny name and a peculiar concept (looking backward to look forward), but History for a Sustainable Future is predicated on the idea that in order to fully understand the social, political, economic, and ecological context of contemporary environmental problems, we need to be conscious of their histories. Resolving local and global environmental quandaries requires careful thought and planning; future success depends on a deeper appreciation of the past. This is the point: historicizing sustainable and unsustainable futures is based less on the notion that we should learn from past mistakes, but rather on the premise that solving the environmental crisis will demand the most and best information available, and history provides valuable insight into the creation and proliferation of the environmental ills we hope to curb.

Frank Uekötter's *The Greenest Nation? A New History of German Environmentalism* offers a particularly important perspective for this larger project, especially with respect to how green initiatives have been integrated into national policy practices. Throughout the twentieth century, Germany has been at the forefront of the global green movement. For North American readers, the history of environmentalism is predominantly a chronicle of conflict and opposition. Indeed, in an insightful reading of environmentalism past and present, the historian Donald Worster remarked: "When contemporary environmentalism first emerged in the 1960s and '70s, and before its goals became obscured by political compromising and diffusion, the destination was more obvious and the route more clear. The goal was to save the living world around us, millions of species of plants and animals, including humans, from destruction by our technology, population, and appetites." In reading through *The Greenest Nation?* the surrender of that grand goal might largely be a North American phenomenon. The only solution to the environmental crisis, Worster claimed, involved the radical recognition that limits to population, technology, and appetite were necessary.[1] Through the twentieth century, a deeper appreciation of the limits to growth has received considerable attention in many parts of Europe. In Uekötter's treatment, the German case is more about cooperation and collaboration. Yes, tensions exist, but the oppositional "us versus them" that typifies North American environmental debates over conservation, pollution, public health, and energy is comparatively absent.

Ueckötter is quick to further stress the distinction between the German example and the traditional environmental narrative that is almost cookie-cuttered into many national histories. German environmentalism was not a knee-jerk reaction to some environmental catastrophe, which spurred the country into a green awakening. Certainly, there is a rich German literature on green issues, but there is no *Silent Spring* that transformed the intellectual and political landscape. Nor were charismatic leaders central to the rise of German environmentalism; Ueckötter points out that Germany's most internationally recognized environmentalist, Petra Kelly, "was much despised and ridiculed among fellow activists and isolated within Germany's environmental community years before her violent death in 1992."[2]

That is not to say that Germany's green movement simply was (the greenest nation was not built in a day). Rather, its historical development might sound familiar to those well acquainted with green initiatives in other countries, though one might ascertain that Germans practiced a more sensitive response to risk. According to Ueckötter, Germany's green narrative had three catalysts. First, that old chestnut post-materialism played some role, though Ueckötter seems less convinced than many of his environmental history colleagues. Where previous generations struggled for material security and balance, Ronald Inglehart's "silent revolution" consisted of coming to terms with taking economic stability for granted and paying more explicit attention to quality of life issues.[3] Second, health—public and individual—galvanized growing environmental interest and concern. Cancer, and the uncertainty surrounding health threats posed by pollution, raised global concerns, but the responses in Germany and its neighbors are telling. What is evident is that northern European countries have traditionally been more willing to apply the precautionary principle to their environmental policies. Third, green politics have been shaped by changing economic contexts. The decline in industry made opposition to its pollution more acceptable and popular. Since World War II, ideas of progress at all cost and stressing the economy over the environment have not held up well in the German context. One might also consider the closed and centralized nature of German politics created space for concerns to be raised on a statewide level.

On a very basic level, we might turn to the German practice as a model for less environmentally enlightened states. And in so doing, *The Greenest Nation?* provides a valuable analysis and template. But that is not enough. Rather than appointing German policies as a prototype for future global environmental decision-making, we need to dig deeper. Too many factors, not least the three above, make the German case an admirable one, but one that is less applicable to other states in the future. This is especially important since Uekötter's work offers an important lesson to environmental historians in the manner in which he situates environmentalism in German history. In effect, *The Greenest Nation?* positions German environmentalism as nothing less than a national code of conduct.

But, as Uekötter rightly argues, even a history of German environmentalism is also a global history—one that is tied to peace and social justice initiatives. And this is an important feature of sustainability: it suggests the comprehensive nature of realizing a greener future. But sustainability also implies hope. Given how easy it is to lose heart at the scale and scope of environmental problems in front of us, I think this is more important than I can ably state. Furthermore sustainability demands a plan, a goal, a mission. And it has been incredibly effective at initiating dialogue. If we can take a hopeful message away from *The Greenest Nation?* it is that history does offer us a means of engaging with a more sustainable future.

Acknowledgments

Every book has its history, and syntheses usually have a particularly circuitous one. After two decades of researching and writing on many aspects of environmentalism in Germany and elsewhere, a book of this kind was a somewhat logical project. It was also an exercise in self-restraint. It probably would have been easier to write a *long* history of German environmentalism, and I am still remorseful about the many stories and people that I have left out: one of the great charms of environmental movement history lies in the fact that it is full of real characters. However, brevity has the salubrious effect of forcing authors to get to the point, and while that made the narrative rather dense at times, it was probably a worthwhile endeavor. I am particularly grateful that I could publish this synthesis in a series that encourages reflections on the present and the future, something that environmental historians have always done and should do more.

In a book of this kind, readers inevitably wonder where the author stands on environmental issues, and I will make no bones about my background here. I am a long-standing member of several environmental NGOs, I have attended and talked at many environmental meetings, and I have done scholarly work for the German ministry for the environment, the Bavarian Bird Protection League, and the Bavarian League for

Nature Protection. I usually buy organic food and pay climate compensation for my air travel. My concern for environmentalism comes from two insights, namely that it is a necessity in our age and that it is fun (at times). And yet for all the enthusiasm that I can bring to green causes, I have had a nagging feeling for years that environmentalism is in crisis and that this crisis defies standard recipes, if not our present ideas about what environmentalism is. My personal conclusion was to opt for critical reflection, a stance that has gotten me into all sorts of trouble over the years (both for being too critical and not critical enough) but still strikes me as the proper role for the environmental humanities. I am also not very good at advocacy.

Many people have shaped my ideas about environmentalism over the years, and that makes a complete list of influences somewhat difficult. The book probably would not exist without the Rachel Carson Center for Environment and Society, which I helped to build as deputy director. For a global institution situated in Munich, Germany, the tension between international and national perspectives is a recurring issue in discussions at the center. I was blessed with clever students who took part in my courses and lectures at Munich University. In a project that deals with the future of environmentalism, one can barely hope for better company than young people who disagree.

Segments of this book were originally published in German as part of my book, *Am Ende der Gewissheiten. Die ökologische Frage im 21. Jahrhundert*, published in 2011 with Campus. I would like to thank Tanja Hommen and Campus Verlag for allowing the reuse of the manuscript, Thomas Dunlap for translating it into English, and the Rachel Carson Center for paying the bill. Claas Kirchhelle, Christian Möller, Kevin Niebauer, Veronika Schäfer, Sarah Waltenberger, and Amir Zelinger read the final draft and provided helpful comments.

Jennifer Thomson gave the text a thorough reading as to substance and style. Series editor Michael Egan and Clay Morgan and Dana Andrus of MIT Press shepherded the project calmly but firmly toward the finishing line. The Volkswagen Foundation supported my work through a generous Dilthey Fellowship.

I dedicate this book to my wife Simona. After all, spouses are the hidden heroes of book writing: they tolerate a distracted and sometimes grumpy partner, they carry an excessive share of household duties, and they prevent public health hazards by insisting that, oh yes, that mug needs washing. Simona has endured that fate more often than I wish to remember, and yet she still shows a genuine interest in my work. The issues of this book have been our household conversation for years on end, and Simona is providing feedback with the vigor of an engineer who meticulously stress-tests complex technological devices—which, incidentally, is her daytime job. She let me know years ago that she would not need a dedication, and that was before I devoted my last book to a snake. But, hey, let's face it, darling: you really earned this.

1

Environmentalism and Environmental History in the Twenty-first Century

The Land of (Organic) Milk and Honey: An Inspection

In a way, this book is an outgrowth of many conversations that I have had over the last years. As a German environmentalist traveling abroad, I have frequently encountered a sense of envy: man, you have it so good! Strict laws, world-class green technology firms, the phase-out of nuclear power and a powerful green party—observers from other countries have come to watch German environmentalism with a mixture of admiration and awe. In May 2012, the Organisation for Economic Co-operation and Development (OECD) called Germany "a laboratory for green growth" and praised its "proactive role in environmental policy within the EU and internationally."[1] In a status report on renewable energy, Mohamed El-Ashry of the United Nations Foundation credited German energy policy with "beacon-like character for many other countries around the world."[2] As a tribute to Germany's green energy efforts, the *New York Times* has adopted *Energiewende* in its vocabulary, along with older terminological imports such as *Kindergarten* and *Schadenfreude*.

These voices match with sentiments in Germany. Environmental problems have long dominated political and social debates, and they usually carry the air of commonsense issues.

Politicians rarely spat over environmental issues, and if they do, they fight over tactics rather than principles. Parties from the left to the right strive to claim green credentials, eager to avoid any kind of statement or gesture that the public might construe as a sign of deficient awareness. A powerful network of nongovernmental organizations represents environmental issues on all political levels, often in close collaboration with state and municipal agencies. All the while, journalists of diverse stripes cover environmental issues in a generally sympathetic light. When it comes to Germany, it is not easy to *not* be green.

A wide array of campaigns, laws, and institutions attests to this mood, making it tempting to compile an impressive list of achievements. In the 1970s, Germany developed one of the largest antinuclear movements in the Western world. During the 1980s, the fear of widespread deforestation turned Germany into the vanguard of pollution control. After the Rio summit of 1992, Germany became a leader in the global fight against climate change. Most recently the boom of renewable energy from wind and solar has galvanized attention around the globe. Of course, a lot remains to be done for environmental sustainability, but as Western societies go, Germany stands out. Even President Obama noted the German clean energy achievements in his 2012 State of the Union address, urging the United States to emulate this example.[3]

However, there is more to the Green Germany than a record of achievements. Over the last two or three decades, being green has emerged as a matter of national identity in Germany. It is hard to explain the enthusiasm for green technology or the fancy for recycling, along with the diligence in separating trash, without a reference to patriotic sentiments. Germans routinely expect their government to assume a leadership role in international negotiations, and few things offend Germans more than being told that another country is doing more for the environment. Given the painful history of German nationalism, one might find that an ironic state of affairs. It almost seems as if, at the end of a long and circuitous road, Germans have finally found a type of patriotism that is truly safe.

The Green Germany has provoked a number of divergent interpretations. A friendly reading suggests that Germans have reached a level of environmental awareness that other countries are still lacking. A less friendly reading suggests a link to the dark chapters of German history, with the Nazi era providing the most popular point of reference. Or perhaps the age of Romanticism continues to resonate within the German soul? Monocausal readings of this kind draw on clichés and are easy to disprove, and yet they have proved hard to exorcise. It is disheartening, to give just one example, that people continue to discuss Anna Bramwell's allegation of a "green party" in Nazi Germany even though scholars have long shown that the quality of her evidence stands in inverse relation to the level of excitement.[4] While German environmentalism attracts worldwide attention, its history seems to attract those in search of a cheap provocation.

This makes it important to clarify the record, and that is what this book intends to do. Most crucially, it seeks to overcome the strange disconnect between German environmentalism today and its history. In most Western countries, environmentalism has grown over time, with different ideas, challenges, and policies accumulating on top of each other like layers of sediment. Some of these developments loop back a century or more; others are of recent origin. Some trends were peculiar, the result of specific events or conditions in a certain region; others were characteristic of industrial societies around the globe. In any case, environmentalism is not something that we can understand by looking only at the last few years. It has deep roots in history that we neglect at our own peril.

It only takes a look at the size of this book to understand that this endeavor is not comprehensive. At the risk of stating the obvious, Germany is a large and diverse country, and environmentalism is a large and diverse movement. The following treatise is as simple as possible but also as complicated as necessary, seeking to identify the main factors and forces in the development of German environmentalism while keeping its distance from intellectual monoculture. The goal is to give non-German readers a general idea of the path of German environmentalism, providing them with a road map that may stimulate more in-depth inquiries. However, while working on the manuscript, it gradually dawned on me that this book would also need to pursue some wider ambitions.[5]

A Time for a New History

Once upon a time it was easy to write a history of environmentalism. All that one had to do was search for key thinkers, authors of influential books, and founders of key organizations, arrange them in chronological order, and then recount their stories in a sympathetic vein. Almost half a century ago Roderick Nash wrote a book of this kind, published it under the title *Wilderness and the American Mind*, and thus created one of the first classics of environmental history.[6] It is still an exciting book, full of stories that both environmentalists and American patriots can read with a sense of pride. Scholars followed the same path for other countries, and nowadays we have books for countries from Great Britain to Israel.[7] For Germany, readers can choose among half a dozen monographs.[8]

It goes without saying that these books were important for the development of environmental history. They showed that there was indeed a long history of environmentalism that deserved closer scrutiny, and presented an outline of that history that scholars subsequently discussed and refined with great merit. However, as research advanced and the number of books and essays multiplied, scholars started to look at these books with a growing sense of disaffection. It became less and less convincing to write the history of environmentalism as a story of "prophets and pioneers," as one title proclaimed.[9] The reasons were both scholarly and political.

Monographs of the 1970s and 1980s typically presented the environmental movement as a rising star. They described environmentalism as a movement that had grown from humble beginnings into a major force that held the promise of a better, greener tomorrow. More recent events have taken much of the air out of these emphatic projections. Two decades after the Earth Summit in Rio de Janeiro, where global warming and biodiversity were the key issues, climate change and the extinction of species continue at dramatic speed, and many other problems remain unresolved as well. When leaders reconvened in Rio in 2012, the enthusiasm of the 1992 summit was only a distant memory, as many observers charged the meeting for producing little more than hot air. Opinions obviously differ on the future of environmentalism, but it is clear that teleologies of an impending green utopia have come to ring hollow. No longer can we write the history of environmentalism as the predestined rise of the greens.[10]

During the last two decades, scholars have also taken a closer look at the choice of people that an earlier generation of environmental historians put center stage. Many of these figures looked rather ambiguous upon closer inspection, and Germany provides a case in point. The first generations of German environmentalists included many people that were elitist, nationalist, racist, or anti-Semitic, and quite a few were all of the above. Every other finding would have been in fact surprising: German environmentalism was never an idealistic sect, far removed from the rest of society, but rather a cross section of the general population with all its imperfections. A late-coming democracy and two dictatorships begat German environmentalism with several generations of environmentalists that provoke mixed feelings in retrospect: they arguably did important and noteworthy work, but they barely qualify as heroes. The enthusiastic overtones that permeated early publications were gradually fading into the background.

Doubts emerged not only about the chosen people but also about those who were left out. Going through the early histories of environmentalism, one cannot help to notice a certain bias: the best chances for consideration had white bourgeois men who had written a book. What about women, workers, peasants, or ethnic minorities? Since the 1980s the environmental justice movement highlighted the fact that disadvantaged groups carry a disproportionate share of environmental burdens, and once historians were sensitized for this type of discrimination and looked back in time, they made a startling discovery: these groups had been anything but silent in the past. A growing number of scholars are nowadays searching for these voices in order to bring them back in.[11]

But as historians were working toward a larger and more diverse understanding of environmentalism, they encountered a conundrum: where to draw the line? Marginalized groups often combined environmental problems with social, cultural, and economic grievances, an approach quite different from the pure green that many classic environmentalists espoused. But if we take these divergent views into account, don't we end up with a blurry definition where almost everyone can be an environmentalist? Few publications showed this dilemma better than Robert Gottlieb's *Forcing the Spring*, which included figures like Jane Addams who no doubt saw themselves first and foremost as *social* reformers. Two decades after its publication, Gottlieb's *dramatis personae* looks uncomfortably reminiscent of a wish list from a left-leaning activist.[12]

Partisan favor is rarely a good guide in these matters, and certainly not when it comes to German environmentalism. Nature protection provides a case in point, as it by and large tilted toward the political right throughout much of its history. Should we exclude these people from our discussion because environmentalism is a staunchly leftist movement since the 1970s? But if we embrace a wider definition, don't we arrive at an endless series of groups and people with their own distinct understandings of environmentalism? In his recent book on climate change, Anthony Giddens went so far as to doubt the existence of the overall subject: "strictly speaking, of course, there is no green movement—rather, there is a diverse range of positions, perspectives, and recipes for action."[13]

We can avoid some of the worst confusions when we add a certain qualification: environmentalism was first and foremost about *doing something*. Books and pamphlets surely played a role, but in the end, it all came down to one question: How should people change their interactions with the natural world? Every movement must eventually come up with a response, forcing members and like-minded groups to communicate with each other, and these discussions provide the historian with an idea about priorities. To be sure, there is no logical sequence here. Neither did ideas always come first, nor did action simply follow from these ideological premises. In quite a number of cases, the reverse was more realistic: to a significant extent, the philosophy of environmentalism was defined on the march.

However, this approach ends up constraining our perspective on a different front: Does environmentalism have to be a *protest* movement? Environmental issues were also subject to government policies, and that is all the more pertinent in the German case, where a powerful and independent-minded state was always part of the picture. It is in fact often difficult to draw a line between the state and civil society. For example, nature protection had barely begun to emerge as a civic issue in the early 1900s when state agencies were starting to co-opt the nascent movement, and some major environmental NGOs actually go back to government commissions. In the field of pollution control, the proactive role of state agencies was a crucial reason for the late formation of civic leagues.

The state became deeply involved in environmental issues early on, but it remained a distinct actor. State agencies have a penchant for order and control and cherish fixed procedures as an inherent good, and that made them less than flexible in dealing with new challenges. Even more, a bureaucracy's mode of operation is anathema to a vibrant people's movement: the state has the proven ability to lull its citizens to sleep. In short, the government was simultaneously opponent, ally, and rule maker of environmental groups, and that makes it hard, if not impossible to leave it out of the picture.

But even when we add the state to our list of parties, the general picture looks far from complete. After all, environmentalism was about more than leagues, policies, and thinkers: it was about life in its full diversity. In Germany, the imprint of environmentalism is visible in what we eat, in what we wear, in the way we move around, and so forth. Being an environmentalist is also about eating vegetarian food, banning the corset, riding bicycles, and countenancing many other things that have shaped the interaction between humans and the natural world in the modern era. It is high time that we take note of these activities and bring them into our narratives. For a history of German environmentalism, sandals and whole grain bread are no less important than secondhand smoke and nuclear power hazards.

Such a new, enlarged history borrows on a wide array of academic disciplines: political history, cultural history, consumer history, the history of science and technology, and history of the body, to mention just a few. A broader and more encompassing history is bound to bring environmental perspectives more into the academic mainstream, and it is certainly more colorful, more diverse in terms of issues and actors, and more open to surprises than a narrative that centers on politics and

NGOs. To be sure, the new history of environmentalism is not simply about an enlarged field of inquiry—it is about a new perspective that should interest every student of German history. This book is not just about a specific issue but also about opening a new window on the past in order to come to grips with the present. What it meant to be green, in a particular place and time, says a lot about what it meant to be German.

Students of German history will surely find many things that ring familiar in this book: the powerful state, the strong sense of regional identity, the change of political regimes, the tension between urban centers and rural livelihoods. But there are also some unexpected twists and turns. The 1950s, often seen as a period of public apathy, witnessed quite a number of vigorous protest movements centered on environmental issues. Civic mobilization even looks more vibrant than during the following decade, notwithstanding the broad wave of discontent that culminated in the events of 1968. After that, it took a rebellious young generation a few years to discover environmental issues, which they subsequently embraced with great success. I will elaborate on all these points in greater detail below, but they may serve to highlight that we cannot study German environmentalism in isolation from other developments. German environmentalism mirrored, and to some extent molded, key issues of German history.[14]

Needless to say, a more inclusive history runs a great risk of getting lost in myriad details. An abundance of issues and perspectives, combined with uncertain narratives, often make for an unstructured morass that is rich in facts and poor in insights. Thus, drawing on the sociology of Pierre Bourdieu, I propose to look at environmentalism as a set of three distinct fields of activity: a field of civic activism, a field of government policy, and a field of culture and life (*Lebenswelt*). Of course, these fields cannot be studied in isolation. Many events in the story at hand touch on two or even all three fields; the founding meeting of the Green Party in 1980, to give just one example, was a civic and political watershed as well as a display of alternative lifestyles. But each of these fields possessed a distinct rationale: specific rules that govern the interaction between people, artifacts, and nature. A clever mode of behavior in the civic field may prove disastrous in policy and culture, and vice versa.[15]

The great advantage of this approach is that it provides the historian with three frames of reference. For each field, we can identify rules of accepted and inacceptable behavior, and we can analyze when, how, and why these rules were changing. Most crucially, we can better account for the fact that environmentalism often comprised strange and even contradictory trends. Generally speaking, the boom times of environmentalism were when all three fields were in sync and reinforced each other; the 1980s, when civic groups, environmental policy and alternative lifestyles all flourished in Germany, provide the best example. However, asynchronous developments in the three fields were the more common situation, and armed with Bourdieu's approach, we can study these divergences and the ensuing tensions in a sophisticated manner. Seen from such a perspective, the history of environmentalism is about distinct rules of behavior in civil society, politics, and culture and their change over time.[16]

Of course, these rules are not deliberate constructs. They have firm roots in cultural traditions, political customs, and interests. In fact Bourdieu encourages questions as to the underlying interests, and these are all the more significant since environmental historians have often given them short shrift. In present narratives, we read far less than we should about the interests of property owners, of experts and scientific disciplines, and of state officials. I would even see one of the key reasons for the rise of German environmentalism in that it tied up with vested interests in a way that served mutual interests.

It is only through bureaucratic self-interest that we can explain the great irony of environmental policy, namely that the massive expansion of regulation occurred precisely at the time when the nation-state was coming under pressure. While globalization and shrinking growth rates were gnawing away the resources of national bureaucracies, environmental issues provided one of the last chances to achieve a massive expansion of budgets, mandates, and staff.

One drawback remains: Bourdieu's fields are strongly defined through the barriers of the nation-state. His defining monograph, *Distinction*, focuses exclusively on France and its peculiar brand of social stratification.[17] However, when it comes to environmentalism, the national frame of reference is a dubious one at best. Rachel Carson, the *Limits to Growth*, the Rio Summit of 1992—a large number of events resonated across national boundaries, creating networks and shared experiences that no history of environmentalism, and certainly not a self-proclaimed *new* one, can ignore. Recent research in fact suggests that there is nothing like a "zero hour" in this international exchange: environmentalism has *always* been international.

German History in the Age of Global History

In 1909, Hugo Conwentz and Carl Fuchs, two leading German conservationists, went to Paris for the first conference on the protection of the countryside. These were tense times in the relation between the two countries. Five years earlier, France had forged the Entente Cordiale with Great Britain, a strategic alliance that Russia had joined in 1907. A number of colonial conflicts were simmering in Africa, and the French had not forgotten the German annexation of Alsace-Lorraine in 1871. And yet the conference proceeded in a most amicable fashion. The French hosts gave the German delegation a particularly warm welcome and invited Conwentz to chair the first session. His presentation, held in French, stimulated lively discussion among the participants. At the concluding banquet, the president of the convention called upon the French government to create an organization after the German model.[18]

Bringing together conservationists from six European countries, the Paris conference highlights an important feature of nature protection before World War I. People all over the West had barely started when they looked beyond their nations' borders at what other countries were doing. Learning from the neighbors emerged as a popular approach to environmental problems, resulting in a lively exchange of ideas and people on a wide range of issues. When Hamburg built one of the first sewer networks on the continent, it hired an engineer from England, William Lindley, a student of the pioneering sanitary reformer Edwin Chadwick.[19] In the United States, Progressive Era reformers looked toward the Old Continent while wrestling with the environmental challenges of urban industrial society.[20] Starting with Royal National Park in Sydney, Australia, countries around the globe were emulating the American model of national parks for the preservation of nature.[21]

Environmental historians have only recently started to explore these international networks and their impact, but this much is clear already: it has become dubious to focus narrowly on a single country. Developments in Germany resonated beyond its borders while international events shaped German debates and solutions, and neither is very surprising on second glance. After all, many countries faced the same kind of challenges since the nineteenth century: pollution, loss of habitats, transformation of landscapes, and so forth. The twin processes of industrialization and urbanization made for an unprecedented set of environmental challenges, and as societies tried to come to terms with them, looking abroad was a matter of common sense.

The case for international perspectives is even stronger when we move up to the present. Since the 1970s, the transnational dimension of environmentalism is about more than conferences and debates. Like most countries in the world, Germany signed numerous international agreements that set limitations on and guidelines for national policies. Furthermore Germany is obliged to heed directives from the European Union, which became a powerful agent on environmental issues in the 1980s and now defines policies on issues from nitrates to global warming. In fact EU decisions shape environmental policy more thoroughly nowadays than many other political fields, making it difficult, if not impossible, to judge German achievements on their own terms.

To be sure, Europeanization has not created a uniform continent. Germany continues to differ from other EU members, and the reasons deserve careful scrutiny. And yet the growing importance of European initiatives underscores the need to write the history of German environmentalism in a broader setting. We should look at German events in the context of international developments, keep an eye on common issues, and trace the impact of German debates and decisions abroad. As it turns out, the imagination of German environmentalism was already global a hundred years ago. In 1914, Augustin Friedrich Krämer, an ethnographer and physician with the German navy, proposed to turn the pacific island of Palau, which was part of the German colony of New Guinea, into a nature reserve.[22]

The colonial dimension of German environmentalism has received growing attention from historians recently.[23] Postcolonial studies have challenged historians in general, and in the case of Germany, interest grew to such an extent that it amounted to a rediscovery of the country's colonial past. And yet it seems that generally speaking, the exchange with the Global South was less significant for the trajectory of German environmentalism than the exchange with other Western countries. For all the importance of colonial and postcolonial fantasies, they pale in comparison with the forces of industrialization and urbanization that Germany shared with other European and North American nations. Therefore this study argues that German environmentalism belonged to a Western type of environmentalism, which turned into a North American and Western European brand after 1945. All things considered, the situation behind the Iron Curtain was notably different from that in the West, and so was the situation in the colonial and postcolonial world.

However, we cannot ignore the situation in Socialist Eastern Europe entirely, as the German Democratic Republic (GDR) was part of that distinct political orbit from 1945 to 1989. At the same time, it is difficult to bring the GDR into a general history of German environmentalism, and particularly so in a study that seeks to trace the historical roots of the present situation. Most GDR traditions, institutional and otherwise, were brutally severed during reunification in 1990, which was by all means typical of the way in which the merger of the two German states took place. Given the disastrous state of the East German environment in 1989, that looked like a well-deserved fate, and the environmental toll of Socialism has inspired a veritable "disaster school" of Eastern European environmental history. However, a number of scholars have recently argued that this approach is exceedingly simplistic.[24] Environmental initiatives in the GDR suffered from a number of drawbacks, with the absence of an independent civic movement surely being the most important one. But East German citizens did speak up, at times with admirable candor, and environmental problems were one of the issues that energized the dissidents during the 1980s. The GDR did also have a serious environmental policy, and some of its measures even exceed those of the Federal Republic. One could even speculate that some fields, particularly nature protection, would be doing better nowadays if West German environmentalists had listened more to their East German cousins.

The GDR makes the story of German environmentalism more complicated; but we can also see that as an advantage. Due to its location, its geographic diversity, and its tumultuous twentieth-century history, Germany includes a good part of what European environmentalism had to offer in the twentieth century: transnational exchange and nationalist isolation, democracies and dictatorships, autarky dreams and welfare states, planned economies and neoliberal deregulation. Germany did not come first on most developments—that distinction usually goes to England—but it was not far behind, making it both recipient of ideas and model for others. It had both Fascist and Socialist regimes, but neither lasted so long as to become the single defining factor in the history of the twentieth century. It is a country of coal and iron, science and engineering, industrial chemistry and forestry, and even a hydraulic nation, as David Blackbourn showed in his masterful *The Conquest of Nature*.[25] In short, Germany is probably the closest thing to a microcosm of Western environmentalism that we can find in Europe.

A history of German environmentalism should thus make forays into international affairs, and I have framed the following story in this way. In doing so, I found that a broad international context is also helpful in defining environmentalism, at least in some broad outlines. For all the differences among industrialized Western countries, we do see some common ground in the understanding of what environmental problems are: pollution, the protection of species and natural treasures, nuclear energy, and so forth. We will take this joint Western agenda as our compass in the following, and we can safely do so if we keep in mind that it is an anachronistic agenda. For most of the twentieth century, these problems were discussed separately, and it is only since about 1970 that they

have merged under the broad roof that we call environmentalism. We can still identify tensions under that roof, such as in
conflicts between wind power and the preservation of species
and habitats. From a historical perspective, environmentalism
is a delicate amalgam, and it is a bit of a mystery why it is so
enduring.

To be sure, an anachronistic term is not inherently prob-
lematic. A good part of the historian's professional vocabulary
is anachronistic: no one talked about an industrial revolution
when it got under way in England. What is more, it is by all
means characteristic that environmentalism grew out of diverse roots—most social movements do. The protest history
of the modern era is full of split-ups and mergers, strange alliances and feuds, and that makes any hope for eternal stability
elusive. It is quite possible that some issues, notably climate
change, may emerge as hegemonic in the future, marginalizing
other challenges in a way that could lead to the disintegration
of our understanding of environmentalism. However, for the
time being, it seems best to work from where we stand.

A Model for the World?

A book of this kind inevitably evokes a certain suspicion,
namely the intention of eulogizing the German achievements.
Surely no author would bother to write such a book if he didn't
think that other countries could learn something from the German experience. And given the widespread praise for Germany's green credentials, it might appear inevitable to conclude
on an emphatic note: Germany as a model that other countries
should copy as best they can. If foreigners and Germans are
equally enthusiastic about the country's environmental record,
it surely must have done something right.

It would be easy to respond to the notion of the Green Germany with a counter narrative that highlights the country's

ecological sins. There is certainly no lack of those. Germany produces some 45 percent of its electricity from coal, and more than half of that comes from lignite coal, one of the most carbon-intensive fuels per amount of energy. It has confined most of its rivers into tight straitjackets. Until Fukushima, Germany was number four in terms of electricity generated from nuclear reactors, behind the United States, Japan, and France. Germany excels in producing high-powered cars that consume wasteful amounts of fuel. It is the only civilized country with no general speed limit on its divided highways—though when driving on the Autobahn, with cars darting along the left lane at breakneck speed, one may doubt that Germany is a civilized country.

It is easier to highlight these liabilities than to say what they mean. In his environmental history of France, Michael Bess stressed the ambiguous results of environmentalism, arguing that it had transformed the country into a "light-green society." The continent's first national ministry for the environment, a penchant for the countryside, but also for nuclear power, a transformation in industrial production methods that reduced pollution but remained energy intensive: in France, achievements and enduring challenges stand uncomfortably next to each other, and Bess concludes that his book "is fundamentally about ambivalence."[26] It would be easy to compile a similar list for Germany. But how do we merge such an ambiguous and contradictory set of findings into a comprehensive assessment? How do we avoid sounding like the clueless teacher who gives all his children the same advice: namely that they have done well but could do better? It would seem that thinking about the overall impact of environmentalism in terms of ambivalence and ambiguity ultimately ends up at a rather unsurprising conclusion: neither France nor Germany, nor any other country of the industrialized West, is even close to sustainability.

Environmental achievements are notoriously hard to define, as they fall in completely different categories: pollution, energy consumption, biodiversity, and so forth. However, there is also a second complication at play here, and that is the diversity of nature. Located in central Europe, Germany enjoys peculiar conditions that frame the overall balance. On the positive side, German woodlands are amenable to management practices that have proved disastrous in other parts of the world. On the negative side, Germany has rivers that run through several industrial regions in a row, causing pollution to build up. Mother Nature is inherently unjust, and that makes it difficult to do justice to a country's environmental profile. The issue of lignite coal, one of the great environmental liabilities in Germany, provides a case in point: How do we account for the fact that many countries do not burn lignite because they do not have any?

Thus, in order to evaluate German environmentalism, it is more satisfactory to think in terms of *environmental potential*. Every country has specific conditions that frame environmental decisions. Some of them are natural: the climate, the extent of woodlands, lakes, and streams, and so forth. Others are human-made, such as the prevailing industries and land use patterns. For environmentalists, these conditions are the point of departure, as they define the key challenges and the range of potential approaches. If we take the German case by way of example, we can see some conditions that spell trouble from an environmental perspective: a high population density, a large industrial base, and winds that are almost always burdened with pollution from neighboring countries. But it also has possibilities: strong administrations, a vast community of scientists and engineers, and a powerful network of environmental NGOs. Every environmental agenda needs to take these basic parameters into account.

Of course, environmental potential is not just a given. The leaps and turns that characterize the history of German environmentalism provide ample evidence for the changeability of context. Conditions in society and the natural environment change, people discover new problems, and policies gain a life of their own. As we will see, some booms of German environmentalism overwhelmed even the activists. It is only in hindsight that we can identify synergies and missed opportunities, and that is precisely why the concept of environmental potential is so rewarding for a study of history: it draws attention to the range of options that countries possessed and whether they used them.

What all this comes down to is that *having* environmental potential and *using* it are two different things. Conditions in a certain country *can* offer a certain solution, but it is by no means certain that the country *will* take that path. Countries may waste opportunities for environmental improvement, they can push limits and achieve dramatic gains, and they can do a lot of things somewhere in between. In short, thinking in terms of environmental potential leads us to a new, more rewarding set of questions. Rather than pondering the question of whether Germany is better than its neighbors, it brings us to ask whether, when, and to what extent Germany realized its possibilities.

If we summarize the overall situation around 1914, there is certainly ground to attest that Germany did an impressive job. Nature protection had inspired an expanding network of state agencies and civic leagues, and cities had built large municipal agencies to deal with the environmental perils of urbanization. But at the same time, the achievements remained below Germany's potential on a number of points. Civil servants and engineers eyed each other suspiciously despite the fact that state power and technological sophistication were a promising combination for many environmental challenges. German officials were also hesitant to accept innovative approaches to new problems, eager to maintain control and their traditional privileges. It is quite telling that American city governments eventually found a more efficient strategy in the fight against the urban coal smoke nuisance than did German administrators.[27] Germany was also apathetic when it came to the efficient use of fossil resources, a key issue of the US conservation movement.

After 1914, two world wars and their aftermath defined German history for decades, severely curtailing the room for environmental initiatives. To be sure, the picture was not completely bleak. The nature protection movement eventually recovered from the standstill during World War I and won a conservation law in 1935 that was probably the best of its age. Biodynamic agriculture emerged in the mid-1920s and became a permanent alternative to chemical farming. Dust control, heretofore a low-tech endeavor, turned into a burgeoning field of engineering. And yet these were isolated achievements, devoid of synergies and a common identity. By the mid-1950s, few people would have thought of Germany as an exemplar country of environmentalism.

Since that time, we can witness a growing number of initiatives that laid much of the groundwork for today's Green Germany. Expert commissions came into being, laws were enacted, and since 1970, ambitious politicians started to tout new environmental programs, making environmental protection (*Umweltschutz*) a household term within a matter of years. But still, few of these measures impressed observers abroad: Germany was merely part of an international wave of environmental concerns. Issues and priorities mirrored trends across the West, and while US environmentalists were fondly recalling the Earth Day celebrations of 1970, the most spectacular events that German environmentalists could offer were a few violent clashes over nuclear power. That changed only in the 1980s when Germany suddenly turned into an environmental leader: strict laws against pollution, the stellar rise of the Green Party, and a broad environmental sentiment in large parts of the population put activists in other countries on notice. When environmentalism flourished globally in the late 1980s and early 1990s, culminating in the Earth Summit of 1992, Green Germany became the subject of global admiration.

That situation was certainly too good to last, and in many ways, Germany is still living off dividends from a fortune that it built during those years. To be sure, green issues remained on the agenda, and German environmentalism was spared the repeated backlashes that characterize US environmental history. Still it is remarkable how much of what environmentalists admire about Germany stems from the 1980s: powerful NGOs, committed state governments, alternative consumerism, green technology. At last Germany had found a way to combine government power and engineering power, thus realizing an environmental potential that had languished for decades. Seeing the international acclaim for eco-friendly research and development from Germany nowadays, one cannot help but wonder why green engineering did not emerge any earlier.

One can thus tell the story of the Green Germany as a tale about a spectacular latecomer: a country that, after spending much of the twentieth century wasting its environmental potential, finally got its act together. Or that would have been the picture two decades ago, for we cannot ignore that the fierce green fire of the 1980s is no longer glowing all that brightly. An economist might invoke the law of diminishing marginal utility: the ecological 1980s allowed spectacular advances for a while, but eventually ran out of steam. In any case, it would seem that environmental progress is more of a piecemeal affair recently. All three fields of environmentalism are still vibrant, but they no longer speak to each other in the way they used to. Whereas civil society, government policy, and culture had reinforced each other during the 1980s, they now look more like autonomous, self-contained fields. Talking with German environmentalists, one can easily identify a sense of crisis—but also a gnawing uncertainty as to what this crisis is really about.

An Open-ended History

Needless to say, this is an assessment for the time being. Predictions are always tricky, and particularly so for environmentalism, which has survived more than one obituary over the years. It would in fact seem that the future of environmentalism has become particularly hard to guess in recent years. When I started to work in earnest on this book project in 2009, the stagnation of environmentalism was plain. Two times in a row, national elections had made the Greens the smallest of five parties in parliament, and the sitting government was bound to expand the lifespan of Germany's nuclear reactors. Toward the year's end, global environmentalism suffered a crushing defeat at the Copenhagen climate summit. Two years later, the same national government reversed its nuclear policy after the Fukushima disaster and pledged to make the transition toward sustainable energy sources. In elections in the southwest German state of Baden-Württemberg, the Green party won almost a quarter of the votes and now runs the country in a coalition with the social democrats. Another two years on, the situation was changing again. When this manuscript was going to press in 2013, worries about costs and side effects were clouding the prospects of renewable energy, and the German solar industry was in deep trouble.

In short, German environmentalism is in a state of flux, and that is probably more than a national peculiarity. In many countries, we are currently witnessing a major transformation of environmentalism: groups and affiliations, habits and lifestyles, policies and ways of thinking change to an extent that we have not seen in a generation. If we are lucky, we are witnessing the birth of a new environmentalism: more transnational, more in flux institutionally, more open to other issues, less idealistic and more pragmatic. If we are not so lucky, we will end up with greenwash and a network of aging environmental NGOs.

The new environmentalism will probably be so different that it defies the terms and concepts that we currently have. It is not clear whether environmentalism will be the defining concept ten years from now. Actually it is not even clear whether that would be a good thing.

In the absence of an endpoint that frames the narrative, a history of German environmentalism is inevitably standing on slippery ground. It would be misleading, then, to present the Green Germany as the culmination of history—the best environmentalism that Germany ever had. It is more appropriate to talk of environmentalism in midpassage, as the Green Germany is currently in a process of change and adaptation to new challenges that many industrialized countries are facing. As the concluding discussion will show, some of the key problems in this ongoing transformation result not so much from the weaknesses of German environmentalism but from its strengths.

Given this background, it is rewarding to approach Germany as a kind of laboratory for the future: what does the German case say about environmentalism in the twenty-first century? Here we have a country that has done a lot of what environmentalism as we know it demands: it has a strong network of NGOs, a green party of international fame, a well-nurtured cluster of green businesses, and a wide range of politicians from the left to the right who like to talk about their country's global responsibilities. Now this country is about to deal with what may be the birth of a new environmentalism, setting the stage for a clash between the past and the future. As environmentalism is about to reinvent itself, does it build on previous achievements? Or does it merely bypass earlier concerns? In the Green Germany, tensions between the old and the new are particularly strong, and that could provide some hints as to where environmentalism may be heading in the future.

With that, this book is not so much a study of success or failure. First and foremost, it is a study of *experiences*. German history reveals a lot about the chances and pitfalls of environmentalism in the modern era, and it is currently providing a test case for the tensions between existing and future environmentalisms. More crucial, it is the story of a country that has recently been successful in realizing its environmental potential—though that was to a large extent an accident of history. As far as we know, there was no Hegelian Weltgeist at work in bringing engineers, politicians, and longhaired leftists together in the making of the ecological 1980s. It is only in retrospect that we can identify the different strands merging in a rather fortunate way.

After all, environmental potential is more than a fixed set of conditions. As people explore certain solutions, they learn about opportunities and pitfalls. And while a society follows a certain path, the general situation may change, making shining examples less than useful for other countries: for all its charms, Germany's ecological 1980s are a model only for a bygone era. However, these past experiences do provide food for thought, and also a good dose of encouragement. In the late 1970s, few Germans would have thought that they were on the verge of a green breakthrough: there was merely a gnawing sense of crisis. Perhaps scholars will look back at our own time wondering why people did not realize what the future held in stock? It would not be the first unexpected turn in the history of environmentalism.

2

Creating a Tradition: German Environmentalism, 1900 to 1945

Defining Decades: The Early 1900s

There is no "zero hour" of environmentalism. Humans have pondered their relationship to the natural environment throughout the ages, and a concern for nature is probably as old as human civilization. That puts the environmental historian into a difficult situation in defining the starting point of narratives. All too easily, we end up looking like a hapless archeologist who diligently dissects one layer of sediments only to uncover older traces below. Surely the 1970s and 1980s played a significant role in German and global environmentalism. However, many decisions during those years merely reaffirmed reform efforts during the early postwar years. In order to understand those reforms, we need to have a look at older traditions, some of which go back to the time of the Industrial Revolution—and perhaps much earlier to medieval edicts on meadows and mining and to the aqueducts of antiquity.

It would be shortsighted to flatly ignore premodern traditions. Sustainable forestry, for one, developed out of a concern of early modern state administrations. Medieval cities recognized the need to regulate the environmental impact of certain trades, though solutions often faltered due to the cramped conditions inside the city walls. However, it seems unwise to go back too far in history in an inquiry that seeks to illuminate the historical background of today's German environmentalism. When we look across the set of institutions and mindsets that exist in the twenty-first century, it is quite clear that most of them are results of the twin challenges of industrialization and urbanization. During the nineteenth century, and particularly during its final decades, we see an intensification of debates and reform efforts that laid the foundations for what we nowadays call environmentalism. The years around 1900 were a watershed in environmental history that transformed basic patterns in the interaction of the human and the natural world. After the closing decades of the nineteenth century, questions about nature, pollution, and other environmental issues looked fundamentally different.[1]

That was the situation in all countries that experienced rapid industrialization and urbanization during the long nineteenth century. As the motherland of the Industrial Revolution, England had a head start, and Edwin Chadwick became the first international star of urban sanitation around the middle of the century. In 1864 the Yosemite Valley in California was placed under protection, followed in 1872 by Yellowstone National Park as the first national park in the world. The Sierra Club, today one of the most important American environmental organizations, was founded in San Francisco in 1892, and the Society for the Preservation of the Wild Fauna of the Empire, created in London in 1903, continues its work in the twenty-first century as Fauna & Flora International. The debates and activities intensified in most Western countries in the decades around 1900, and we see the beginnings of an international conservation network, for example, at the International Conference for the Protection of Nature in Berne organized by the zoologist Paul Sarasin in 1913. Thus something akin to a transnational consensus was already visible on the eve of the First World War. Ever since, a country's affiliation with

Western civilization hinged on some conscious efforts to protect nature.

How did the efforts in Germany look against this background? What were the specific characteristics of German environmentalism in its nascent stage? The first thing that stands out is its huge diversity. While wilderness became a guiding principle of the US preservation movement, in Germany there never existed a general, authoritative idea of nature in need of protection. Some people dreamed of large national parks, while others focused on small plots and natural monuments; some were concerned about unspoiled nature, while others were interested in cultural landscapes or individual species like birds. This diversity of motivations inspired an equally complex network of groups and individuals. For example, the League for Homeland Protection [*Bund Heimatschutz*] founded in Dresden in 1904 pursued the protection of nature as part of a broad effort to cultivate regional traditions. By contrast, the Association for Nature Protection Parks [*Verein Naturschutzpark*] founded in 1909 pushed for the creation of large protected areas. The State Office for the Protection of Natural Monuments [*Staatliche Stelle für Naturdenkmalpflege*] pursued a third path in the state of Prussia: under the leadership of the scientist Hugo Conwentz, it set its sights on small-scale objects such as spectacular trees and rocks.[2]

Some initiatives achieved enormous popularity in a regional context. The membership register of the Isar Valley Association [*Isartalverein*], established in 1902 by the architect Gabriel von Seidl, soon read like a "Who's Who" of Munich's cultural scene. Likewise the Association for the Protection of Alpine Plants [*Verein zum Schutz und zur Pflege der Alpenpflanzen*] set up by the Bamberg pharmacist Carl Schmolz soon attracted wide support and recognition. Occasionally, however, the creation of an organization tended to be the starting point for a lengthy search for identity: one example is the 1898 Münster

Association for Bird Protection and Canary Breeding [*Münsteraner Vogelschutz- und Kanarienzucht-Verein*], which, after four name changes, operated as the Westphalian Association for Nature Protection [*Westfälischer Naturschutzverein*] from 1934 on. Three years later there was yet another change to Westphalian Natural Science Association [*Westfälischer Naturwissenschaftlicher Verein*], a name it has retained to this day.[3]

A plurality of organizations was certainly no German peculiarity. For instance, the creation of separate associations for the protection of birds fits into an international pattern: the League for Bird Protection [*Bund für Vogelschutz*] had powerful counterparts in the United States in the Audubon Society and in England in the Royal Society for the Protections of Birds, with women playing a central role. Lina Hähnle, the wife of a Swabian industrialist, led the German League for Bird Protection for almost forty years, a tenure that would seem hard to top until one realizes that Winifred Duchess of Portland ran the Royal Society from 1891 to 1954. No other animal species gained such an agile lobby, and the champions of bird protection often became shock troops that blazed paths for other conservationists. For example, Israel's environmental movement grew to a significant extent out of the battle for the Chula valley in northern Galilee, which was important for migratory birds.[4] However, bird protection generally had a difficult time of it in the Mediterranean region, where hunting and eating songbirds was a tenacious tradition, especially since the northern neighbors across the Alps attacked this "bird killing" sharply and with tones presuming a superior level of civilization. Most people had forgotten that roasted lark and bird soup had been on the menu in Germany into the nineteenth century as well.[5]

The networks of associations and institutions was so complex that environmental historians are still struggling to come to terms with it. The geographic diversity of the Reich, combined with the individualism of the German states, led to an unusual degree of fragmentation. There was also the quintessential German penchant for unproductive scholarly debates, which soon led to countless disputes, all the way to veritable skirmishes. For example, the homeland protection organizations strenuously opposed the creation of honorary committees in the Prussian provinces, by means of which Conwentz sought to promote his protection of natural monuments. Conwentz, for his part, schemed against the large preserves of the Association for Nature Protection Parks. His predilection for small-scale protection was, in turn, derided by Hermann Löns, in a famous quip, as "conwentzional nature protection": "The despoiling of nature works 'en gros,' nature protection 'en detail.'"[6] From the very beginning, then, there was a cheerful conflict over divergent conceptions, which soon became a permanent feature of the conservation debate. In theory, a rich reservoir of ideas could also be an asset, but most conservationists thought otherwise.

Still, notwithstanding all the quarrels and disagreements, an institutional network developed in the two decades before World War I that remained remarkably stable for decades. Many of the organizations created at that time have played an important role to this day. The League for Homeland Protection continues to exist as the League for Homeland and Environment [*Bund Heimat und Umwelt*], while the League for Bird Protection gave rise to today's NABU (short for *Naturschutzbund Deutschland*). For more than a century the Association for Nature Protection Parks has worked for the Lüneburg Heath; the Bavarian League for Nature Protection [*Bund Naturschutz in Bayern*], founded in 1913, is today the largest environmental organization in that state and, moreover, was godfather at the founding of the German League for Environment and Nature Protection [*Bund Umwelt und Naturschutz Deutschland*, or BUND] in the 1970s.

The prevention of cruelty to animals has an even longer tradition. The first German association appeared as early as 1837 in Stuttgart, and it also works for animal protection to this day. In 1879, some organizations merged into the League of Animal Protection Associations of the German Reich [*Verband der Thierschutz-Vereine des Deutschen Reiches*]. In 1913, 222 of the 413 German animal protection organizations were corporate members.[7] The animal protection movement in Imperial Germany grew in similar fashion, but it also changed in a less than edifying way: animal protection showed overlaps with the anti-Semitic movement through the criticism of Jewish kosher slaughtering, far more so than in England, the motherland of the animal protection movement.[8]

For all the differences of opinion, there was at least one consensus: the protection of nature was based on a protection of *land*. This may not seem very remarkable from the perspective of the twenty-first century, but things looked different before 1900. It was arguably the most important innovation that distinguished nature protection around the turn of the century from previous traditions. The nineteenth century did not lack appreciation for nature, but it did lack the idea that this involved property rights and areas under state protection. Thus the many beautification clubs of this era were mostly concerned with an esthetically pleasing look of nature: they planned and built paths, green spaces and fountains, monuments and observation towers, always with the intent of prettying up the natural landscape for locals and tourists. It was by all means characteristic that the Beautification Association for the Siebengebirge [*Verschönerungsverein für das Siebengebirge*], founded in 1869, initially avoided conflicts with the operators of quarries and focused instead on opening up the mountains to tourism. Only when a new Association to Save the Siebengebirge [*Verein zur Rettung des Siebengebirges*] pushed aggressively for a prohibition of landscape-destroying quarries, did the Beautification Club begin to take an interest in area protection. By 1914, the club was able to purchase around 800 hectares of land and to put a stop to destructive uses. In 1922, the Prussian government declared the Siebengebirge a nature reserve.[9]

The trend toward the state-guaranteed protection of certain areas was evident in all Western countries, and that suggests that this change was not so much about new ideals of nature as about a new understanding of state power. From this perspective, the rise of nature protection was a by-product of what the American historian Charles Maier has called the "age of territoriality."[10] Maier argued that the reach and efficiency of nation-state bureaucracies took on a new quality in the late nineteenth century in all Western countries. The railroad had revolutionized surface transportation, and telegraph networks made it possible to communicate in no time at all. As a result governments were able, for the first time, to subject all parts of their territory to regular and uniform control. Only that control made conservation areas a realistic option in the first place: what would have previously been an empty gesture for lack of enforcement could now be credibly mounted and implemented.

Nature protection as it emerged around 1900 was therefore unthinkable without an alliance with state authorities. In the case of Germany this alliance was particularly strong: there was hardly another country in which state administrators reacted as quickly and decisively as they did in Germany. This is apparent from a comparison with the United States and Great Britain, countries that, together with Germany, spawned the largest nature protection movements at the turn of the century. In the United States, more than half a century passed from the first protective mandates for the Yosemite Valley to the creation of a separate federal agency in 1916. It was only from this time on that an institutional guarantor of protection and professional management existed in the National Park Service.[11] The British parliament supported the work of the National Trust for Places of Historic Interest or Natural Beauty (founded in 1894) by enacting a law in 1907 that declared its acquisitions to be inalienable. Great Britain went further in its colonies, but on the British Isles the state's administration remained emphatically reserved until the Lower House passed the National Parks and Access to the Countryside Act in 1949.[12]

This kind of restraint was foreign to German officials. The newly created civic organizations had barely begun working when the state administrations were already eagerly searching for ways to pull the new issue into the orbit of state policies. The Grand Duchy of Hesse-Darmstadt, in its 1902 Law for the Protection of Sites of Historic Interest, considered the protection of natural monuments and their surroundings, while the Prussian parliament passed its first law against the disfigurement of scenic areas that same year. Beginning in 1905, the State Committee for the Preservation of Nature in Bavaria [*Landesausschuß für Naturpflege in Bayern*] assembled a broad array of associations under the auspices of the state administration. Württemberg pursued a similar path after 1908 with its State Committee for Nature and Homeland Protection [*Landesausschuß für Natur- und Heimatschutz*], which quickly set out to create committees in the state's sixty-four counties. In 1906, Prussia created the State Office for the Protection of Natural Monuments, which, as an organ of consultation and scientific research, was under the direct authority of the Prussian Minister of Culture. More than anything else, it was this State Office and its director, Hugo Conwentz, who shaped the face of nature protection beyond Germany's borders, and the extensive system of provincial and district committees in all parts of Prussia certainly made an international impression. In 1922, a Soviet scientist went so far as to call the head of the Prussian office the "apostle of the humane nature protection movement."[13] A few years later, a Dutch study noted: "Nowhere else in Europe does there exist such an extensive organization for nature protection as among our neighbors to the east."[14]

These activities showed a remarkable open-mindedness on the part of the Prussian-German administration, but also the intention to domesticate the young movement. It is in fact hard to separate these two motivations: precisely those people who advocated nature protection within the administration simultaneously warned—in the style of administrative paternalism—against "exaggerations," as though the conservationists were good-natured children who, unfortunately, got carried away now and then. As a result the nature protection committees were strictly limited to an advisory function, while decisions remained in the hands of the state administration, which usually gave priority to political and economic needs. The League for Homeland Protection learned about these limits the hard way when it launched a campaign to preserve the Laufenburg Rapids, a scenic spot on the Upper Rhine between Lake Constance and Basel, which was under threat from a power plant project in the early 1900s. The Baden Ministry of the Interior remained completely unfazed by the organizations' lists of signatories, which included prominent names like Werner Sombart and Max Weber, and it granted a permit. The only concession was that it commissioned a painter to immortalize the Rapids in oil before their destruction. The painting has been hanging ever since in the Staatliche Kunsthalle in Karlsruhe.[15]

On the whole, the conservationists' alliance with the state came down to a peculiar mix of freedom and impotence: they could criticize everything and decide nothing. It is remarkable indeed what kind of latitude the authoritarian Prussian-German state granted to the conservationists. For example, the only prescribed task of the Prussian State Office was to write an annual report. Likewise the members and directors of the provincial committees were not subject to any mandates. In

Laufenburg Rapids on the Rhine, which conservationists tried in vain to preserve. Picture Staatsarchiv Basel-Stadt.

Baden, nature protection work was even completely delegated to the state's Association for the Study of Nature [*Badischer Landesverein für Naturkunde*], and Saxony did the same with the Association for Saxon Homeland Protection [*Landesverein Sächsischer Heimatschutz*], which in return collected a subsidy of 37,000 Marks in 1912.[16] Bureaucrats clearly saw the nature protection movement as a well-meaning and somewhat naïve partner, and they had no reason to expect any unpleasant surprises from it.

The result was a hybrid of governmental and societal nature protection that did not exist in other European countries. The boundary between a civic organization and bureaucracy became increasingly blurry, and the German conservation movement soon had at its disposal resources and legal instruments of which activists in neighboring countries barely dared to dream. But this alliance came at a price: the closeness to the state increasingly shaped thinking and action. Prohibitions and punishments became the instruments of choice, and nature protection soon appeared quite authoritarian. In an essay, Walther Schönichen, the head of the Prussian State Office since 1922, complained vigorously about letters from citizens that revealed "a certain superficial and amateurish understanding of the concept of nature protection."[17] Only a few took as critical a view of German nature protection's proximity to the state as the ornithologist Leo von Boxberger, who in the 1920s warned repeatedly against the "ordinance-mania of the new-German type." Nature protection that relied above all on the punitive power of the state, he argued, "degenerates only too quickly into petty harassment and arbitrary police behavior, vices to which the bearer of state authority in Germany is all the more prone, the smaller he is."[18]

This mindset was a considerable burden when it came to alliances with other groups. What stands out in a comparison with other countries are the deep reservations German conservationists felt about those seeking rest and relaxation in nature. In France, two decidedly tourism-oriented organizations—the *Touring Club de France* and the *Club Alpin Français*—were part of the network of nature protection.[19] American conservationists promoted visits to the national parks with the slogan "See America First" and support from railroad companies; to satisfy the taste of the Europe-oriented clientele, park concessionaires built chalets in the Swiss style and even dressed service personnel in pseudo-alpine dirndls.[20] In contrast, German conservationists preferred to talk about the side effects of tourism; here the alienation of the Prussian-German state from its society merged with the educated bourgeoisie's aversion to the masses. Those working to protect nature and homeland liked to lament the "carnivalization" of nature, and when it came to ugly billboards, the tone escalated to pure hatred. The most they would accept was solitary hiking in the wild. Everything else was disagreeable "horde wandering."[21]

We can also see the consequences of the closeness to the state in dealings with landowners, an inevitable conflict in densely populated Germany. One approach was to buy up areas worthy of protection; to that end, lotteries worth millions were organized for the Siebengebirge and the Lüneburg Heath, for example.[22] However, this was a cumbersome and time-consuming process, and one that depended more or less on the goodwill of the landowners. As a result conservationists asked themselves whether the alliance with the state might not open up other possibilities. Could one not simply expropriate the landowners, ideally without any financial compensation? Was the situation not really that "the state—as the representative of the general public interest in culture—did no one an injustice if it prevented an individual from depriving those alive now and future generations of an irreplaceable good?"[23] After all, one did not pay respectable citizens for obeying the law. Shortly before the First World War a few prominent conservationists made that argument in a petition to the German governments and called for the legal option to expropriate areas in the interest of conservation without compensation. However, the petition demonstrated awareness that conservation was crossing a sensitive threshold here: it came with the request that the bureaucrats treat it as "confidential."[24] The petitioners sensed that they could not gain such drastic restrictions of property rights in the democratic process. No surprise, then, that this initiative had no tangible result.

Early conservation did not lack issues. It dealt with endangered species and power plant projects, dams and observation towers, picturesque rocks and the use of bird feathers for women's hats, while homeland protectors had their eyes on additional issues, from old buildings to folk dress. However, pollution problems were usually beyond their horizon: conservationists rarely took note of the fact that factories and big cities were fouling the air and contaminating rivers with wastewater. That is remarkable, as problems were hard to deny: in Germany's urban areas, one could literally see, hear, smell, and taste the new time. In 1904, for example, the social democrat Philipp Scheidemann scoffed in the *Reichstag* that the Wupper river "below Solingen is in fact so black with filth that if you dunk a National Liberal into it, you can pull him back out as a catholic Zentrum man."[25] In the Prussian parliament, a speaker from the Rheingau region read a revised version of Heine's poem about the Lorelei, in which the fateful Rhine maid stopped her accustomed singing out of protest against the smoke.[26] But such complaints did not lead to vigorous association work, let alone the creation of special organizations, a situation that we can register as the third peculiarity of the German environmental movements in the early 1900s. The vigorous activity of nature and homeland protection stood in striking contrast to civil society's apathy in the face of pollution.

The situation was different in other Western countries. In Great Britain, for example, several organizations existed: the Manchester and Salford Noxious Vapors Abatement Association was set up in 1876, a Coal Smoke Abatement Society devoted itself to fighting London's legendary smog since 1898, and the rest of the country fell within the purview of the Smoke Abatement League of Great Britain after 1909. These associations pushed authorities and polluters into action, at times helped by their own staff of inspectors. After the victory over the London smog, the Coal Smoke Abatement Society became the National Society for Clean Air, which changed its name once again in 2007; since then it has been operating as the world's oldest organization of its kind under the name Environmental Protection UK.[27] In the United States, as well, civic reform associations were indispensable in the battle against smoke and soot, with women playing a significant role. On the continent, such associations were rarer, to be sure, but at least there were organizations like the Austrian Society Against the Smoke and Dust Nuisance [*Österreichische Gesellschaft zur Bekämpfung der Rauch- und Staubplage*], which published its own newsletter after 1906. But Germany lacked a comparable organization.[28]

To be sure, there was considerable anger about smoke, soot, and other visible pollutants in Germany. Women of one Frankfurt neighborhood circulated a proposal "that the entire neighborhood should go on a protest march to city hall to show them our cleaning rags," but such a demonstration never materialized in Frankfurt or elsewhere.[29] Urban reform organizations were equally apathetic on the issue. And when farmers and foresters complained about damage from acidic gases, they were in most cases merely eyeing generous monetary compensation.

The reason lay in the attitude of the authorities, which behaved very differently toward pollution problems than they did toward conservationists and homeland protectors. After all, pollution was a matter of order and public health, and thus touched on a core task of the police. In countless statements and decisions, the German authorities made clear that wherever threats to health or unacceptable conditions existed, there was a need for a remedy—and that was that. Officials were decidedly allergic to public discussions about their course of action, no matter which side was voicing discontent. Even from business circles, criticism was tolerated at most in minute doses. When business people, at a meeting in 1899, carped about the implementation of rules and regulations by technical laypeople, one Berlin factory inspector declared gruffly: "I take exception to the manner in which judgments have been passed on the implementation of the smoke ordinances by the police."[30]

Tough talk was one thing, however, and enforcement quite another. Authorities sometimes sprung into action, but they were far from exerting systematic control. For all their good intentions, they were severely overtaxed: there was a lack not only of oversight but also of clear directives. How, for example, should one recognize the "intolerable conditions" against which, in the conventional view, one had to take action? Since neither threshold values nor analytical methods existed for most problems, the work of the bureaucracy was often quite makeshift: one fought against what could be avoided with simple measures and declared all other pollution as "acceptable" and "locally customary." In quite a few instances one could also sense the desire of the officials to legally constrain themselves as little as possible so that they could respond flexibly in case of complaints. And so the bureaucracy tried to muddle through with improvisation and compromises, and this had the effect of channeling and neutralizing a considerable part of the public discontent: anyone who was suffering from unusually high pollution could obtain some relief if he spoke up. That certainly did not solve the overall problem, but it blunted the protest.[31]

Tense relations between state officials and engineers were part of the problem. There were not only different ways of thinking at stake here but also divergent interests on the job market. Since jurists had a monopolistic hold on the general administration, only subordinate positions were open to technical experts—something the professional associations of engineers protested against tenaciously and unsuccessfully. This situation had severe consequences because the fight against pollution problems increasingly required technical knowledge and engineering solutions. In theory, the rising group of German engineers would have been an ideal complement to the strong state; in practice, however, no one talked about such an alliance around 1900. Engineers were adamant that they did not work in this field "to set the lever of legislation in motion."[32] The idea that only regulatory edicts could clear the path of technological progress was almost unbearable for the proud engineers of Imperial Germany.

The rise of bacteriology made the situation even more complicated. By medical criteria, smoke and dust were merely a nuisance rather than an actual threat to public health, and the same was true for many effluents of industry. While sanitary reformers had initially pushed numerous environmental issues with a broad concern for health, they came to favor a more constrained vision of disease under the influence of bacteriology. As a result sanitary attention focused more and more on the provision of clean water and the secure disposal of sewage and waste, and city administrations spent considerable sums on such provisioning and disposal networks.

Late-nineteenth-century cities invested heavily in sanitary infrastructures, and they were proud of it. As this engraving shows, the city of Hamburg invited notables to take boat rides through its sewers.

City governments were at their best when a municipal company could solve the problem. Thus the late nineteenth century saw the creation of a broad spectrum of municipal institutions: waterworks, slaughterhouses, garbage collection, gas and electric utilities, as well as garden agencies that looked after municipal parks. Cities in fact became so important as corporate service providers that contemporaries spoke of "municipal socialism," and only a few dogmatic liberals found this kind of socialism offensive.[33] The reputation of these capable and relatively corruption-free municipal corporations soon extended beyond the German borders. American urban reformers made their way across the Atlantic in droves to watch, at times with tears in their eyes, a German sewage treatment plant.[34]

Of course, the power of city administrations had its limits. When it came to problems like noise and air pollution, where little could be achieved by creating municipal corporations, they mostly floundered. Urban planning, too, did not get off the ground until the twentieth century. On the whole, however, municipal administrations invested in urban infrastructure on a massive scale, and here Germany was firmly part of a European trend: cities from Paris to Budapest were competing for the latest and best urban technology. The city dwellers of Central Europe are benefiting from this legacy to this day: city parks, roadways, the reliable disposal of waste—the quality of life and the attractiveness of the European metropolises rest not least on accomplishments from the turn of the century. It usually takes a trip abroad for Europeans to realize that these things are not simply a given.

Municipal services required not only large investments but also clarity on many technological issues. What, for example, was the best way of dealing with human sewage: should one store it in cesspools and haul it to a dump in regular intervals, or simply flush it away with the city's other effluents? Discussions over these issues took place at the meetings of the

Association of the Lower Rhine for Public Sanitation [*Nieder-rheinischer Verein für öffentliche Gesundheitspflege*] and the German Association for Public Sanitation [*Deutscher Verein für öffentliche Gesundheitspflege*]. Founded in 1869 and 1873, these two organizations illustrate a fourth characteristic of environmental discussions in Imperial Germany: the strength of scientific expertise. This was not surprising at a time when German academia held worldwide acclaim, and a long list of achievements attests to Germany's pioneering role. At the Saxon Forestry Academy in Tharandt, Adolph Stöckhard demonstrated around 1850 that sulfur dioxide was noxious to plants and, in so doing, established an internationally renowned tradition of smoke studies.[35] The first academic journal dealing specifically with air pollution appeared in 1910 under the pretty title *Rauch und Staub* [Smoke and Dust]. The arm of German science had a long reach: Prussian academia was even involved in the creation of the State Office for the Protection of Natural Monuments.

It thus made perfectly good sense that German nature protection had a strong scientific bent from the outset. To be sure, in Germany scientists were never as dominant as they were in Tsarist Russia, where the *zapovedniki* protected areas were simultaneously objects of scientific study. But German researchers were strong enough to form a potent faction within the broad spectrum of conservationists. Their diligence found an outlet in long list of species, and it is characteristic that the very first conference for the protection of natural monuments in Prussia in 1908 had "inventories" on the agenda (not without a pithy comment that existing publications were not in accord "with the principles laid down by the minister").[36] At times the connection was also reflected in institutional affinities: the conservation commissioner for the province of Westphalia, for example, had his office in the Museum of Natural Science in Münster, and in Baden the State Collections for Natural

Science served simultaneously as the state's office of conservation. From the very beginning, though, the scientization of conservation was an ambivalent trend: it secured a high level of professionalism, but it also made communication with the rest of society even more contentious.

The quest for personal well-being and closeness to nature did not remain limited to politics, however. Both were central to the Life Reform [*Lebensreform*] movement, which grew into an important part of bourgeois life in Imperial Germany. The Life Reformers were a truly colorful crowd: sartorial reformers fought against the corset, teetotalers and vegetarians advocated new diets, naturopaths presented themselves as an alternative to conventional medicine, and the *Wandervogel* hiking groups whipped the German youth into shape. Educational reformers founded boarding schools out in the countryside, "air and light baths" invited participants to engage in *Freikörperkultur* [nudism], and in 1893, a meeting at the vegetarian restaurant Ceres in Berlin-Tiergarten decided to set up a fruit garden colony named Eden near Oranienburg, where the comrades soon indulged in gardening work dressed in white linen garments. (Later on, they became more moderate and carnivorous.)[37]

Life Reform alternated between provocative sectarianism and popular liberation, and that makes it difficult to pinpoint its significance. It revolved around lifestyles, around a person's own body and its health, and believed that the transformation of society would arise primarily from individual change. Thus politically, Life Reform was noncommittal: one could buy whole grain bread and consult naturopaths without having an inkling about the fate of the Laufenburg Rapids or the Lüneburg Heath. On the one hand, Life Reform nourished ideas about the garden city and mixed urban planning, and in this regard it made a significant contribution to urban development in the twentieth century. On the other hand, it certainly had a whiff of escapism: the ecological horror of the industrial age was pretty far removed from the Oranienburg Eden. However, Life Reform surely demonstrates that the yearning for nature was more than a political demand. Closeness to nature and a healthful way of life became popular ideals beyond bourgeois circles.[38]

All told, then, one can identify five ways in which turn-of-the-century German environmentalism stood out in an international context: a great diversity of guiding ideas and associations, the key role of a proactive administration, the absence of civic organizations in conflicts over pollution, the early development of scientific expertise, and a colorful Life Reform movement, which accorded nature a tremendous significance in how people lived their lives. These characteristics are all the more important in that they would leave an imprint on German environmentalism throughout the twentieth century. Even the events of the postwar period did not push these traditions into oblivion.

So were the environmental movements of Imperial Germany a strong movement? An answer is difficult because contemporaries rallied around concepts such as nature, homeland, and hygiene, rather than environmentalism. This is more than a terminological problem, as these notions reflect divergent understandings of the problems and, not least, divergent enemies. Some fought against polluting industry, and others against the excesses of modern culture; some condemned the big city while others wanted to make it more salubrious. And these divergent approaches reflect in turn the fissures of German society: the tensions between the business community and the intelligentsia, the unresolved social question, the tension between hegemonic Prussia and the other states, the gulf between urban and rural society, and the crisis of a political system that acted, in Max Weber's famous metaphor, like a runaway steam train. In short, the environmental movements of Imperial Germany were individual movements without a common identity.

Nature protection, in particular, looks like a contradiction in itself: a social movement full of individualists. This made for a diverse and colorful movement, but also for a lot of friction.

Compared with other countries, Germany did reasonably well. It had renowned sanitary reformers, strong municipalities, a state bureaucracy conscious of its powers, and a broad spectrum of influential, well-connected organizations. And yet the picture is ambiguous: power and impotence were often merely a matter of perspective. Germany had scientific experts for smelter smoke when other countries were just beginning to grasp the problem—but in the end, their advice usually amounted to deals behind the scenes. The big cities spent a lot of money for clean drinking water—but the investments remained for the most part hidden under ground, and innovations like the water closet were soon taken for granted. And all the enthusiasm of the conservationists could not, after all, cover up the fact that nature and homeland protection remained for the most part a phenomenon of the elites. Even the League for Bird Protection, probably the most popular organization in its day, did not exceed 41,000 members before 1914. It all came down to a set of paradoxes: the environmental movements of Imperial Germany were influential and fragmented, popular and misanthropic, scientifically competent and without strong allies, close to the state and constrained for that very reason.

Judging merely by the intensity of the debates, Imperial Germany can stand comparison with the period after 1945. The only difference was that before 1914 there were few signs of a broad environmental movement in the making. It was unrealistic to expect that the fault lines and conflicts would miraculously disappear over time. And yet there was one experience that united all these movements: the feeling that things were moving forward. From Life Reform to air pollution control, from scientific research to nature and homeland protection: in every instance one could discern a long-term trend toward the better—often even a veritable boom—that filled members and activists with enthusiasm. However, this boom came to a sudden and brutal end in August of 1914.

Times of Crisis: World Wars, Weimar Years, and the Nazis

The First World War was a painful turning point for most social movements in Germany. Wartime mobilization was merely the prelude to a decade of violence, misery, and death, which came to a temporary conclusion only with the end of hyperinflation in 1923. A few years of relative stability, promptly glorified as the "Golden Twenties," gave way to the Great Depression, Nazi rule, and World War II. European historians increasingly see the period from 1914 to 1945 as a distinct epoch: Eric Hobsbawm, in his global history of the twentieth century, speaks of an "age of catastrophe."[39] For thirty years, crises came thick and fast, in all sorts of ways: military, political, socioeconomic. It is little surprise that these years were not a good time for environmentalism, either.

Once people realized in the fall of 1914 that the war would not end with a swift victory, meetings were canceled, projects and publications were postponed, and activists went into collective hibernation. Nature protection was henceforth a private pleasure, for which some members of the educated bourgeoisie found time and leisure even during military service. In 1916 the journal of the Bavarian Botanical Society published an essay about "the death of spruce trees caused by artillery shells"—a bizarre showcase of what academics do in total war.[40] The total mobilization of resources for the war effort made peacetime concerns appear like luxuries. Even the federal government held in 1918 that "among the factories created during the war there are some that so poorly comply with requirements for the protection of neighbors and workers that their speedy shutdown is desirable."[41] When a resident of Erfurt complained about nighttime noise from an engine factory, a medical official, who had been consulted as an expert witness, responded that the petitioner should "thank God that he is not suffering any nuisance from our enemy during the current war."[42]

After the armistice in November 1918, there were some encouraging signs with regard to the legal situation. The Weimar Constitution was the first German constitution that took the protection of the natural environment into consideration, and the 1920 amendments to the Prussian Field and Forestry Law [*Preußische Feld- und Forstpolizeigesetze*] permitted "regulations for the protection of animal species, plants, and conservation areas," and it was henceforth referred to as the "little conservation law."[43] But these were ultimately open-ended promises that stood alongside ominous developments in the open countryside. The shortage of food during World War I spurred efforts to cultivate unused land, which often had special ecological value. In early 1924, the Prussian government even entertained the idea of closing down the Institute for Water, Soil, and Air Hygiene, the supreme scientific authority on pollution issues in Prussia since its foundation in 1901, for the purpose of budget consolidation. A wave of protest from municipal authorities stopped the closure.

The "Golden Twenties" were hardly any better for conservationists. A special source of frustration was that neither Prussia nor the national government passed a conservation law, even though the Prussian parliament had explicitly called upon the government to do so.[44] Only smaller states like Anhalt, Mecklenburg-Schwerin, and Hesse enacted conservation laws during the Weimar years. In Berlin, the attempt of the ambitious Brandenburg Provincial Commissioner Hans Klose to get the proletarian masses excited about his own cause with a People's League for Nature Protection [*Volksbund Naturschutz*] came to naught. After ten years of work, the League had a measly 2,000 members.[45] Among the few winners of the Weimar years was the Bavarian League for Nature Protection: from a mere 537 in 1918, its membership had risen to 18,086 by the end of the Weimar Republic and continued to grow also in the Nazi state.[46]

It therefore comes as no surprise that conservationists were fairly indifferent to the fate of the Weimar Republic during its terminal crisis in the early 1930s. Parliamentary democracy had done little for conservation on balance, and bitter political conflicts were not to the taste of its clientele. Nothing illuminates the apolitical self-conception of the nature and homeland protectors better than the "Appeal against the blighting of the appearance of the homeland from excesses of election propaganda" that the German League for Homeland Protection published on the occasion of the federal elections in July 1932. Others feared the rise of the Nazis or the violence in the street, but homeland protectors were concerned about electoral canvassing "that completely ignored any consideration for the appearance of the homeland." "Decisive measures" were called for to counter these "previously unknown bad practices": "The German people, however, can and must expect deference to the homeland."[47]

On the local and regional level, conservationists did achieve some notable successes. For example, a petition drive saved the Laacher See in the Rhineland from a hydroelectric project in 1926.[48] However, the most spectacular event of the Weimar years was a by-product of one of the great crises, the French occupation of the Ruhr region in 1923. Germany reacted with civil disobedience, and with industry mostly shut down from spring to fall, the region experienced a dramatic improvement of air quality during the growing season. The results were spectacular: vegetation recovered with amazing speed, gardeners witnessed plant growth like never before, and farmers were bringing in bumper crops. It was a real life simulation of what the region would be without pollution, though one that few felt like repeating: for the people along the Ruhr, economic standstill brought hardships, starvation, and the near-collapse of the Weimar democracy. Except for Mother Nature, civil disobedience had only losers.[49]

Some promising developments grew out of the wave of rationalization in the 1920s, though their importance is evident only in hindsight. The severe shortage of coal during and after World War I spurred the development of fuel economy as a new branch of engineering, thus elevating resource conservation from obscurity. In an economy striving for autarky, dust was increasingly seen as a valuable raw material, and the building of filters evolved into a booming sector of the economy. The Association of German Engineers [*Verein Deutscher Ingenieure*, or VDI] set up an Expert Committee on Dust Technology in 1928 "to bring together these efforts and promote scientific work."[50] The Expert Committee developed quickly into a lively meeting place for engineers and other experts: in 1937, for example, a general meeting attracted 260 members and guests. The VDI was vigilant about technical discussions and emphasized that members acted "not as representatives of agencies, organizations, or companies to which they belonged, . . . but as experts, even when an agency or company had proposed them as members."[51] While this sounds a bit naïve in retrospect, it had a disciplining effect in that the debates focused on scientific issues and not, for instance, on the manufacturers' latest products. This was thus the first time that officials, experts, and industry representatives came together in what was emphatically called "cooperative work." It was a precedent for the corporatist style of regulation that would become one of the pillars of German environmental policy after 1945.

There surely was an urgent need for efficient dust filters during the interwar years. The trend was toward large electric power grids with huge central power stations that burned coal with great efficiency but at the same time spewed vast amounts of ash from their smokestacks. The use of pulverized coal became particularly infamous for its fly ash problems. In 1927, the power plant of the Mont Cenis mine near Herne caused a scandal when it polluted its surroundings on a scale that was excessive even by the standards of the Ruhr. Officials ran out of patience: if the nuisance did not disappear soon, "we will shut the place down." The mine quickly set about to build a dust-filtration system and promised that it would "faithfully review" damage claims.[52] From the 1930s on, large power plants were built with ash filters from the outset. Controversies abounded over cleaning efficiency, though, as costs rose exponentially with every percentage point of efficiency.

Meanwhile, agriculture saw a conflict that led to the development of "biodynamic" cultivation as an alternative to conventional agriculture. In June 1924, Rudolf Steiner, the founding father of the philosophy of Anthroposophy, delivered eight lectures on the "spiritual foundations for the renewal of agriculture" at the Kober estate near Breslau.[53] They provided the impetus for the creation of an Agricultural Research Group that quickly attracted attention beyond Anthroposophist circles. The biodynamic method was not actually all that new: it drew on classic humus management practices and a holistic view of the farm as an organism that had been part of the standard repertoire of agricultural science since the late eighteenth century. However, the Anthroposophists simultaneously demanded the renunciation of artificial fertilizers, a staunch provocation for agrochemistry, which had been among the key disciplines of the agricultural sciences in Germany since the time of Justus von Liebig. At the same time, farmers were sympathetic to this point of view, as investments for artificial fertilizers were among the largest expenditures of farmers in the 1920s. And, to top things off, Anthroposophists suggested that artificially fertilized plants were of inferior quality or even carcinogenic without presenting evidence. Agrochemistry replied with a no-holds-barred campaign. Irate experts spoke of "heresies," "sham science," "99 percent humbug," and "a fanaticism that would make you think you had been thrown back into the darkest days of medieval ignorance." When the Nazis came to power, representatives of the agricultural-scientific establishment called openly for tough measures against these "charlatans."[54]

In the end, the year 1933 saw only regional laws muzzling the biodynamic farming method, and these were repealed after some time. However, this was only the beginning of twelve turbulent years in the wake of which biodynamic agriculture became in equal measure a victim of Nazi persecution, the hobbyhorse of Nazi grandees, a playground of autarky policy, and an accomplice in the policy of annihilation. In the beginning it was Rudolf Hess who protected alternative farmers and prevented a ban on biodynamic organizations. After 1940, the Nazi minister of agriculture Richard Walther Darré, already de facto stripped of power at this time, took an interest in the biodynamic method, which he later made part of his defense strategy in the Ministries Trial after the war. From 1940 on, Heinrich Himmler had the biodynamic method practiced at several experimental farms of the SS, among them an infamous herb garden at the Dachau concentration camp.[55]

This contradictory history was quite symptomatic of the fate of environmentalism in Nazi Germany. It was not "National Socialism" as such that was at work here, but rather diverse sets of individuals and groups, and their standing was subject to violent swings. As a result there is hardly an issue where we can discern a consistent policy over the twelve years of Nazi rule. In the very first months, the Nazis passed a far-reaching animal protection law, but they immediately watered it down when physicians protested. Following the Nazis' accession to power, Werner Haverbeck aggressively pursued the *Gleichschaltung* in the newly created Reich League for National Character and Homeland [*Reichsbund Volkstum und Heimat*], until the League collapsed in the fall of 1934. In 1934, Hermann Göring shocked the German forestry community when he appointed Walter von Keudell, a supporter of the concept of the "permanent forest" [*Dauerwald*] as the head of the newly created Reich Forestry Service [*Reichsforstamt*]. After three years, the advocates of traditional clear-cutting and the exigencies of war preparations won out, and Keudell made way for a more compliant successor. When it came to the construction of the Autobahn, Fritz Todt, the Inspector General for the German Roadways, employed a cadre of special "landscape lawyers," led by the charismatic landscape architect Alwin Seifert, only to treat their suggestions with lukewarm interest.[56]

Clearly, there was no coherent line on these issues, let alone a systematic environmental policy in Nazi Germany. This point is all the more important since this history has often been written in an exceedingly one-dimensional way. In most cases it was done with the obvious intent of being provocative. For example, in the 1980s Anna Bramwell caused a stir with the argument that a "green party" or a "Steiner connection" had existed in Nazi Germany.[57] Occasionally there were also attempts to interpret Darré's blood-and-soil ideology as a fascist ecophilosophy—which took this ideology more seriously than many a Nazi did. Now and then, Nazi references were also misused in conservation debates as a political cudgel.

Provocations were cheap, but they spurred research and gave rise to what is by now a fairly unambiguous finding: there is no way we can speak about a Nazi permeation of the conservation movement. To be sure, there were various points of connection with the amorphous Nazi ideology, but the rapprochement with the Nazis was ultimately driven by tactical considerations. The Nazi movement, too, never regarded conservation as a brother in spirit, and before 1933 we can hardly discern meaningful contacts between the two movements. Conservation never had much use for core themes of the Nazi program like anti-Semitism and Social Darwinism, and some Nazi initiatives—such as the push to cultivate moorland—aroused the worst kind of fears. One of the first statements of conservation under Nazi rule was an "appeal from the German landscape to the Labor Service" that was penned by Walter Schönichen.[58]

What initially prevailed after the Nazi ascension to power was a sense of uncertainty about what the new times would mean for conservation, and some expressions of loyalty seem quite ambiguous upon closer inspection. For example, in August 1933 the Sauerland Mountain Club [*Sauerländischer Gebirgsverein*] decided at an extraordinary general meeting that "there is no need to adjust ourselves"—a statement that we can also read as a rejection of Nazi plans to remake the conservation community.[59] The attempted *Gleichschaltung* in the Reich League for National Character and Homeland caused uproar among the grassroots organizations, as the fractured conservation scene cherished the autonomy of associations. To move out of the defensive, the German League for Homeland Protection began a campaign against billboards in March 1934, but it was hastily canceled after protests from the advertising industry.[60] Conservationists thus had mixed experiences at best after two years of Nazi rule, and everything pointed toward weary coexistence. But that changed in June 1935, when the new rulers enacted a Reich Conservation Law—a piece of legislation that environmental historian Charles Closmann has called "one of the industrialized world's most wide-ranging conservation laws."[61]

Ironically, this resounding feat was mostly due to chance and personal interests. Support from Hermann Göring was crucial: Göring railroaded the bill through the Nazi cabinet while at the same time making sure that conservation was incorporated into his Reich Forestry Office. This had a lot to do with Göring's stamp-collector attitude toward titles and tasks, but also with his fondness for the Schorfheide north of Berlin, where he ran a quasi-feudal regime around his country estate Carinhall. The Schorfheide Foundation that Göring created ostensibly for conservation purposes in reality served to finance his passion for hunting. Göring took little interest in other nature reserves, but this failed to alert the conservationists. For them, the Reich Conservation Law was the long-awaited demonstration of favor from the very top. "Reich Forestry Minister Göring has now taken conservation into this strong hand and given our efforts the backbone of Reich law," rejoiced the Bavarian League for Nature Protection in August 1935.[62] Three years later the conservation commissioner in the *Gau* Hesse-Nassau emphasized in a circular: "I once more draw emphatic attention to the fact that this conservation law was created at the initiative of the Führer."[63]

The Reich Conservation Law offered nearly everything that the movement had been demanding for decades. It provided for the protection of natural monuments and the designation of nature reserves, dispensed with the diversity of regional approaches and replaced them with a uniform conservation administration for all of Germany, and opened up new possibilities for landscape protection and planning. The authorities were now able to identify landscape reserves, and conservationists were to be consulted on all projects that had a significant impact on the land. There was even a solution to the tricky question of compensation: in accordance with the Nazi principle of "the common good above the individual good," point 24 of the NSDAP's party program, the Reich Conservation Law allowed for the uncompensated expropriation of areas deemed worthy of protection. This was a valuable trump card in the vexatious negotiations with landowners, and the work of the conservationists took on a new pace as a result. Conservation areas were now identified by the dozens, negotiations that had dragged on before were now concluded in record speed, and

Hermann Göring, here seen practicing his passion for hunting, was the key figure in the Nazi boom of conservation. His national conservation law of 1935 won widespread acclaim within the conservation community, although it was ultimately a pyrrhic victory. Picture SV-Bilderdienst.

some of the newly appointed conservation officials worked as though in a frenzy. Even a decade later, Hans Klose, the head of the Reich Conservation Office since 1938, spoke glowingly of this "high time of German conservation."[64]

Klose was not the only one who indulged in nostalgia after the war. In 1949, the Baden conservationist Karl Asal declared that the passage of the Conservation Law had been a "decisive battle": "The progress we owe to it can be truly assessed only by a person who had been involved in practical conservation work already before, and who had to struggle to make do with inadequate legal defenses. With one stroke, conservation, often enough treated with disdain, had become a factor to be reckoned with."[65] The quote shows how the strengthening of conservation had its roots in the alliance with an authoritarian state, which was positioned against a reluctant society. A number of clashes with the National Socialist leisure organization *Kraft durch Freude* [Strength through Joy] revealed how much conservation continued to mistrust the "masses."

The enthusiasm of conservationists bore elements of self-delusion, since the environmental balance sheet of the Nazi regime was obviously negative: the list of sins ranged from ecologically disastrous swamp clearance and river regulation projects to the consequences of the war economy. But for the conservation community, this was only one side of the equation. For a brief period they had actually enjoyed the attention of those in power, and the blessing of the Nazis had allowed a kind of conservation work that had not been possible before or thereafter. For a few years, conservationists could take decisive action in a way that was surely impossible in a democratic state under the rule of law. But at the same time, there was no denying that this had made them complicit in a genocidal regime. Thus what was left at the end of the Nazi years was a mixture of contrary emotions that burdened the work of conservationists for a long time to come. They knew only too well that they had seriously burned their fingers during the "high time."

The first circular that the Reich Office for Conservation sent to conservation commissioners after the war provides insights into the prevailing mindset. "Conservationists to the front," was the motto that Hans Klose used to gather the remaining men around himself: "The only person who is tolerable in our ranks today is the one who has the fanatical willingness to work with all his power for the nature of the homeland."[66] For Klose this was the hour of a manly challenge: "During these months, and surely even beyond the next year, what is at stake are so many and major homeland valuables that not *one* of us must fail."[67] In the midst of postwar chaos, conservationists were thus given a clear motto: close ranks, show commitment, and not a word about the past. Well into the 1950s and 1960s conservationists acted like a sworn community, closed off against a society whose stirrings they followed with suspicion. After the disastrous alliance with the Nazi state, it was best henceforth to only trust each other.

This was not a good attitude for the start of a new era; but at first it did not really look like a new era was coming. All the signs were pointing at restoration: the associations from the interwar period organized themselves anew, old networks were reactivated, and work suspended during the war resumed. New organizations fit seamlessly into the existing structures. The guiding ideas, too, were those of the early 1900s, and so the notion of *Heimat* radiated once again in full glory for a few years—not least because it could serve collective identities that lacked a vocabulary after the word "nation" had been discredited.[68] But didn't everything point toward continuity? Since the turn of the century Germany had a broad range of associations, it had strong laws that remained in force, and the state offices also continued, at least in Western Germany. The Reich Office for Conservation, which had found provisional shelter in the Lüneburg Heath after the end of the Reich, survived as well, and in 1953 it resettled in the new capital of Bonn. There was no rupture in terms of personnel either, and thus everything seemed to favor a continuation of the tried-and-true traditions. It turned out to be the last dance of the old guard.

3

Getting in Motion: German Environmentalism, 1945 to 1980

Dirt and Demonstrations in the Miracle Years

In the collective memory of the Federal Republic, the 1950s have long since taken on mythical status. Total defeat and the miseries of the immediate postwar years gave way to a long boom that entered into common parlance as the "economic miracle" [*Wirtschaftswunder*]. Between 1950 and 1973, GDP grew at an average annual rate of around 6.5 percent, an unusual growth rate even for a time when all Western economies were humming along. While the economy had been a notorious source of trouble in the interwar period, it now became a first-rate guarantor of political stability. Mass consumption became the signature of a new kind of affluent society.

At first glance, environmental problems do not quite fit into this panorama. They seem to belong more to the period *after* the frenzy of consumption, when the costs of the boom moved to the fore of awareness. However, environmental issues gained new prominence already in the 1950s, which is not all that surprising upon closer inspection. From the perspective of the twenty-first century, we tend to associate ecological issues with a critique of consumption and growth. But for the 1950s, the opposite correlation was much more plausible. The environmental problems of that time could still be perceived by the senses: deforestation, dirty water, and dust-laden air. Conditions that people accepted during times of hunger now became subject to criticism, and with that the growing environmental debate was initially not a movement in opposition to the West German economic miracle, but a complementary phenomenon. The environmentalism of the 1950s grew out of traditional German values such as *Behaglichkeit* and *Gemütlichkeit*, a quest for simple pleasures and homely comforts. And, in any case, why should people tolerate the pollution of the environment given that life in general was getting ever more pleasant?

The issues that attracted attention under these circumstances were entirely local in nature. The core concern was protecting one's personal environment against negative impacts, and that gave the protests a special urgency. Furthermore the general climate of the Adenauer years did not exactly invite political mobilization. The Westernization of the Federal Republic had just begun, and manifestations of pluralistic democracies such as demonstrations were still looked upon with skeptical eyes. The old guard of conservation mostly stuck to the traditional procedures of the authoritarian German state and focused on petitions and negotiations behind the scenes. Letters of protest remained the most important instrument, and yet one could sense that the discontent was pushing toward new, more aggressive modes of expression. It was not least environmental issues that transformed the German *Untertan* into a self-conscious, active citizen.

A prime example was the conflict to preserve the Wutach Gorge in the southern Black Forest, which for a time kept an entire region in suspense. It was triggered by a dam project of the Schluchseewerk power company, by which much of the water was to be diverted from the valley of the Wutach and used to generate peak electricity. The Wutach Gorge was a wild, canyon-like river valley that had acquired a reputation as a Romantic natural treasure in the nineteenth century; some dubbed it the German answer to the Grand Canyon. The valley was a protected area since 1939. With that, the conflict was about a valuable piece of nature, and lurking in the background was the question of how much security the designation as a nature reserve really offered. When petitions failed to make an impression, Fritz Hockenjos, the nature conservationist of the Black Forest Association [*Schwarzwaldverein*], founded the Working Committee for Homeland Protection in the Black Forest [*Arbeitsgemeinschaft Heimatschutz Schwarzwald*] in 1953. While this setup had the major advantage that it offered associations from the region the chance to join as corporate members, it was revealing that Hockenjos created a new organization outside of the existing structures to fight for the Wutach Gorge. He obviously harbored doubts whether an established organization would be able to manage a large public campaign.[1]

The dispute dragged on for several years, and both sides fought with the gloves off. The Working Committee attracted attention from beyond the region with posters, brochures, meetings, and active media work, and it gave no hint of any willingness to compromise: "Hands off the Wutach Gorge," was the motto of the movement. As early as January 1954, the State Cultural Agency [*Landeskulturamt*] of South Baden spoke of a "popular movement in favor of preserving the Wutach Gorge."[2] The Schluchseewerk reacted with a flyer that lamented the "propaganda presentations" of the Working Committee.[3] For a protest rally at Freiburg University, the Schluchseewerk even brought in two busloads of workers and employees who made their presence known by heckling, which the Working Committee in turn denounced sharply as "propaganda methods": "These manners are reminiscent of the disastrous brawling methods of a not-too-distant past," thus demonstrating how the Nazi experience resonated in virtually all postwar conflicts.[4] The Working Committee collected no fewer than 185,000 signatures against the dam, a demonstration of where public opinion was standing.[5] In the end, the government and the Schluchseewerk reversed course around 1960 and decided to shelve the project.

To be sure, this conflict still had a good dose of the 1950s' mustiness. The demonstrations of the Working Committee were still fairly diffident: it preferred to organize "excursions" into the Wutach Gorge, and as the culmination of the last great rally in May 1959, the participants joined in singing a popular folksong.[6] We can see a more vigorous approach in northern Germany, where just at this time activists fought to preserve the Knechtsand, a nondescript sandbank in the estuary of the Weser. This was all the more remarkable as the conflict in the tidelands of Lower Saxony led directly into the minefield of cold war defense policy. The threat to the Knechtsand came from airplanes of the British Royal Air Force, which had used Helgoland, a remote North Sea island, as a bombing range after World War II. When West Germany pushed for the return of Helgoland, the Royal Air Force demanded an alternate site, and Knechtsand was chosen. However, this site was much closer to the coast, and so considerable discontent grew in the region. In the beginning the crab fishermen were particularly active, as they suffered economic losses from the restricted military zone. They eventually won financial compensation from the federal government.[7]

The debate took on a new quality when the elementary school teacher and amateur ornithologist Bernhard Freemann made a momentous discovery: the Knechtsand, hard to reach from the mainland and therefore little studied, served as a resting place for Common Shelducks in the summer. The birds spent their molting period there, which left them unable to fly for almost a month and thus rendered them helpless victims of the bombs. In the summer of 1954, Freemann and his comrades-in-arms, who later organized themselves into a Protection and

Research League Knechtsand [*Schutz- und Forschungsgemein-schaft Knechtsand*], found thousands of cadavers. Their discovery quickly turned into a political issue. Was this merely a fraction of the victims, with many more cadavers carried out to sea by the tide? If so, how great were the real losses? Freemann initially spoke of 45,000 dead ducks, soon of at least 70,000, and both figures remained controversial. Could one trust the numbers of an amateur ornithologist, who also had an obvious interest in the most spectacular numbers? This skepticism led to further investigations, the Royal Air Force set up its own Common Shelduck Committee, and only gradually did it become incontrovertibly clear: the Knechtsand was in fact a major European molting site.

As a result the protest acquired a significance that transcended borders. Since the bombs were now a nature protection problem, agencies all the way up to the Federal Office for Nature Protection and Landscape Conservation [*Bundesanstalt für Naturschutz und Landschaftspflege*] took an interest in the sandbank. British bird conservationists became involved, the *Times* of London covered the affair, and the House of Lords discussed it in 1956. Soon memories of the bombing raids during World War II were mixed into the debate, for example, by the *Bild Zeitung*, the leading German tabloid, which put the issue on its front page in October 1954: "A hail of bombs on a German bird paradise." All the while, West Germans were embroiled in a bitter debate over rearmament, and so pacifist groups were suddenly interested in Common Shelducks as well. Representatives of the German Communist Party liked to show up at the meetings. Police officers blended into the audience and took notes.

The protest movement reached its climax on a dreary Sunday in September 1957. The Protection and Research League invited supporters to a spectacular demonstration on the Knechtsand, revealing astonishing skill in dealing with modern mass media. Twenty colorfully decorated cutters ferried three hundred demonstrators and reporters to the island, speakers stood barefoot on a washed-up wooden crate, and above them a large European flag fluttered in the wind; upon their return, torchbearers were greeting the fleet. After widespread media coverage on the demonstration, Freemann and his followers were no longer willing to compromise, and suspending the bombing runs during the molting period only was now out of the question. They demanded that the Knechtsand be declared a nature reserve, and a month later the state issued such a decree. In February 1958 Great Britain declared that it would henceforth refrain from military use of the Knechtsand.[8]

The Wutach Gorge and the Knechtsand were two of numerous conflicts that flared up during the 1950s, albeit some of the most spectacular. To be sure, not all these conflicts ended in victory. The struggle of Bavarian conservationists against hydropower projects on major rivers and cable cars in the Alps, for example, was largely unsuccessful.[9] Nonetheless, it is remarkable that issues that previously would have tended to remain internal administrative procedures were now discussed in public. New was also the dramatic language: the community of Kleinblittersdorf in the Saarland, for example, which was downwind from a large French power plant, called for action by the authorities "before our once flourishing place will become a Pompeii from this devastating ash fall and all human and plant life suffocates in the dust."[10] At the Feldberg in the Black Forest, the community of Menzenschwand fought against a uranium mine over three decades and eventually achieved its permanent closure in 1991.[11] The struggle over the Hoher Meißner in Hesse, a mountain that was a site of memory for the youth movement and which came under threat from a coal mine, ended in 1960 with its designation as a nature reserve.[12] In Lampertheim in South Hesse, a "Save the Palatinate" Committee fought to preserve the Lorsch Forest, where the US military wanted to clear 800 hectares for an airfield. When the Lübeck Police killed ten dogs in a refugee camp because of a rabies scare in 1954, 1,500 dog owners and animal lovers demonstrated against the "St. Bartholomew's Massacre of the Dogs" with a protest march through the city center.[13]

Of course, none of this compares with the citizens' initiatives that sprang up everywhere since in the 1970s. Postwar Germany was still a society with material hardship, refugees, and people in improvised shelters. Even full employment was only attained in 1961, when the unemployment rate dropped below 1 percent. A serious problem was also the sluggish reaction of established organizations, which did not quite know what to do with the bourgeoning discontent. When it came to grassroots work, they mostly thought in terms of slide shows and annual meetings; they were neither materially nor intellectually prepared for supporting a protest movement. As a result the protest found expression mostly in "Emergency" and "Working Committees" that were set up for a particular cause and had trouble putting their work on a permanent footing once a conflict was over. When the guns fell silent at the Knechtsand, tensions within the Protection League grew, and in the end Freemann was expelled from the board and even banned from setting foot on the island. The Working Committee for Homeland Protection in the Black Forest continued to speak out about regional issues like the planning of the Autobahn, but after the battles of the 1950s that seemed like an afterthought. Hockenjos remained active, though, and became president of the Black Forest Association from 1970 to 1979.

The situation was similarly bleak among state agencies. Conservation officials were at best indifferent toward the growing discontent in the general public. When conflicts over strip mining escalated in the Rhineland around 1960, nothing but silence came from the conservation commissioners, of all people.[14] In the Knechtsand conflict, the Federal Office for Nature Protection actually schemed against Freeman—conduct whose motives the environmental historian Jens Ivo Engels has described as "difficult to fathom."[15] Closeness to the state and authoritarian manners, an elitist self-conception and skepticism toward the "masses"—there was no lack of obstacles to the communication between the conservation community and its society. It suddenly became obvious that the extensive network of officials was in fact a giant with clay feet. In principle, it was possible to use the leeway that the office of the Conservation Commissioner offered for aggressive work in close collaboration with civil society, as Otto Kraus, the head of the Bavarian State Office for Conservation [*Bayerische Landesstelle für Naturschutz*], demonstrated. But the activism of Kraus remained exceptional.[16]

Yet conservationists did not lack legal powers. The Reich Conservation Law remained in force after 1945 (though the West German constitution prohibited expropriation without compensation), and thus it depended largely on how vigorously it was employed. In retrospect it is astonishing what could be achieved already in the 1950s when the existing regulations were used to their fullest extent. Even the skyline of the national capital was a product of conservation. When federal ministries in Bonn were flirting with the construction of imposing high rises in the Rhine meadows, the District Commissioner threw up a roadblock by invoking a landscape protection ordinance.[17] Conservation officials liked to complain about a lack of personnel, but that was half the truth at best. The system gave commissioners a lot of leeway in defining priorities, and thus any uniformity in conservation work was illusory. In more than one region, conservation work came to reflect personal hobbies and predilections.

What was lacking in the 1950s was not only an effective integration of the scattered activities but also a plausible philosophy. To be sure, after 1945 there had initially been a renaissance

This map shows some of the places that played an important role in Germany's environmental history.

of the critique of civilization. Once again, intellectuals pondered the "curse of technology" and humanity's Faustian urges. But from the middle of the 1950s on, the gloominess increasingly lifted: a highbrow critique of progress sounded ever more quixotic in the midst of the material blessings of consumer society.[18] This was recognized also by the representatives of conservation, which is why they renounced any antimodernism: as the Sauerland Conservation Commissioner Wilhelm Lienenkämper noted, the intent was "not to bring back the romantic stage coach, but to live fully and completely in our time."[19] In 1947, though, that same Lienenkämper had still spoken very differently before county commissioners of his region: "But is not the deification of technology, the megalomania of humans, and the growing disappearance of awe modern paganism? Have we become happier ever since we have been lifting the veil of creation; ever since we want to be as wise as God and know what is good and evil? Don't we feel as we did at the expulsion from paradise?"[20] The affirmation of modernity by Lienenkämper thus sprang more from tactics than from inner conviction, and other conservationists drew on the classic themes of cultural despair as well. Even Hockenjos bemoaned that he was waging his battle for the Wutach "in a time of unholy materialistic contamination."[21]

Given this mindset, it is not surprising that reform initiatives came mostly from outside the conservation community. Philanthropist Alfred Töpfer challenged the German conservation community with a speech at Bonn University in June 1956 that eventually led to the creation of recreational "nature parks" [*Naturparke*] that exist to this day.[22] Count Lennart Bernadotte, who had a knack for nature and turned the Mainau Island in Lake Constance into a flower park, assembled a group of experts for roundtable talks that proclaimed a "Mainau Green Charta" [*Grüne Charta von der Mainau*] in April 1961, one of the first environmental call-to-arms in the

Federal Republic.[23] In 1958, Günther Schwab published his novel *Der Tanz mit dem Teufel* [Dancing with the Devil], the first eco-bestseller after the war.[24]

Some initiatives yielded enduring results. In May 1955, Heinrich Grünewald, representing Germany's engineers as director of the VDI, and the representative of the VDI Expert Committee for Dust Technology attended a meeting of the Interparliamentary Study Group [*Interparlamentarische Arbeitsgemeinschaft für naturgemäße Wirtschaft*], which was discussing ways to combat air pollution. Shortly thereafter the press reported that a social democratic member of parliament was working on a bill that included provisions for "an independent commission of experts." Grünewald immediately contacted the Secretary General of the Interparliamentary Study Group, Wolfgang Burhenne. The initial motivation was surely negative: the VDI regarded such a commission as an unwelcome competition for its own Expert Committee for Dust Technology; moreover German engineers continued to be averse to politicization. But in their conversation Grünewald and Burhenne developed a positive and quite consequential idea. They decided to forgo laws for the time being and instead focus all energies on the development of technical rules and guidelines. What were the merits of tough-sounding laws if no one knew in the end how efficient the filters had to be? The result was the VDI Commission on Air Pollution Prevention [*VDI-Kommission Reinhaltung der Luft*], which to this day plays an important role in the development of technical standards.

The outcome was as remarkable as the process. It was the elitist politics of the 1950s at its best: two powerful men met for a frank conversation and forged a compromise. The agreement between Grünewald and Burhenne served the environmental interest of the Interparliamentary Study Group as well as the professional interests of the engineers. The latters' desire for independence soon came to a test when the powerful

Federation of German Industry [*Bundesverband der deutschen Industrie*] sought to put the reins on the VDI Commission: after all, the industrialists argued, the issue had "not only technological but, to a significant degree, also economic aspects." The remark touched off the engineers' sense of pride, as they under no circumstances wanted to be seen as the "extension of industry." Grünewald ostensibly stressed the need for a "balanced composition" of committees; furthermore the goal was "to achieve conventions and not to impose regulations on anybody."[25] At the very outset, then, it became clear what a precarious balance the VDI Commission had to maintain—but also, and that is the point, that there were forces that supported nonpartisan "cooperative work." The attitude of state officials which initially eyed the commission's work with suspicion and only slowly came to trust it, strengthened these forces even further. To this day, the VDI Commission serves as a model for the power of German corporatism.[26]

The genesis of the VDI Commission was symptomatic of reforms during the 1950s. Insiders were setting the tone, and they embraced a cautious approach to reform. There was constant vacillation between the desire for changes and the effort to preserve the existing structures as much as possible. On the one hand, the reforms aimed with some skill at the important screws within the administrative machinery, such as guidelines and technical standards. On the other hand, bureaucrats sought to preserve the traditional leeway for decisions and shield processes from outsiders. All the while, civil society stood on the sidelines, a backdrop to reform efforts, but not an active participant in ongoing debates. None of the civic leagues of the fifties showed an interest in administrative structures, and the conservation community continued to think that pollution was not its issue. For instance, Hockenjos and his Working Committee never took much interest in the fact that the Wutach Gorge was threatened not only by a dam, but also by the effluents of a nearby paper mill.

The pollution of rivers was another problem that had been the subject of controversial debates already in the nineteenth century and acquired new urgency in the postwar years. The dismal state of Germany's waterways showed in huge mountains of foam that were floating on rivers and canals in the unusually dry and hot summer of 1959. The federal government responded by setting up an expert commission, whose members included independent scientists, waterworks, and the detergent industry. In this instance, too, corporatism was the method of choice. Nobody was put in the dock; instead, an effort was made to arrive at a solution with everyone involved. But this did not mean that the problems had been put off. In 1961, years before similar concerns were voiced in the United States about the Great Lakes, a law on detergents was passed, which addressed soap components that did not easily break down biologically.[27] The times when one could ignore conspicuous problems with a shrug of the shoulders were over.

Of course, the reformist zeal within the bureaucracy was nowhere near ubiquitous. When it came to air pollution, there was really only one state in the 1950s that took a strong interest in changes: North Rhine-Westphalia. The trigger was the Ruhr region and specifically the Settlement Association for the Ruhr Region [*Siedlungsverband Ruhrkohlenbezirk*], whose director drafted a model law as early as 1952. With increasing affluence, the residents of the Ruhr region, like citizens all over the West, felt that environmental problems were an annoyance. In 1959, a regional newspaper described air pollution as "Ruhr problem No. 1." That same year in Essen-Dellwig, Clemens Schmeck, a Homeopathic doctor and chairman of a civic league, filed an injunction against a nearby steel mill when eye problems were multiplying among the children of his neighborhood. Thanks to this kind of mood, officials were able to proceed much more aggressively. As early as 1954, in negotiations about airborne dust from lignite coal power plants in the

Rhineland, officials warned of "administrative 'self-defense' measures under pressure from public opinion."[28]

The Ministry of Labor and Social Policy became the driver of change. This also reveals quite a bit about how deeply the competencies were fragmented within the German bureaucracy. Given the nature of the issue, one would have expected the interior or economic ministry to take the lead. But the labor ministry was in charge of the factory inspectorate, which had developed into the defining authority on industrial pollution since the turn of the century. The competition with other agencies gave rise to an important self-interest on the part of the ministry of labor: when it comes to defending and expanding jurisdictions, agencies like to go all out. Characteristically, the Labor Ministry acquired new positions and additional funds, and for two decades North Rhine-Westphalia became the pacesetter of air pollution control in Germany.

Emission control thus became a political football already in the 1950s. Still change for the most part possessed the flair of administrative-technical reforms: only insiders understood the true meaning of the Law Amending the Trade Code and the Federal Civil Code, which the Bundestag passed shortly before Christmas in 1959. Only in the summer of 1960 did those in the Chancellor's Office grow nervous and press for a review of additional measures "also in view of the approaching federal elections."[29] Air pollution indeed became an issue in the 1961 election when Willy Brandt declared in his speech at the party convention: "The sky over the Ruhr region must become blue again!"[30] The phrase stuck and became an environmental icon: for most Germans, it is pretty much the only thing they know about air pollution control before 1970. Brandt's phrase was not tied to any concrete political program, though, let alone in notable difference to the incumbent: for politicians of the 1950s and 1960s, strengthening air pollution control was a matter of common sense. From 1962 to 1970, five state air quality laws were passed without a single dissenting vote.

The bigger problem was that reforms of the 1950s and 1960s generally followed the top-down approach that Germany had adopted in the late nineteenth century. Change focused on new laws and guidelines, with the tacit assumption being that they would somehow trickle down. In other words, reform was mostly an elite effort, disconnected from the everyday work of pollution control. Drawing on Bourdieu's theory of fields, we can speak of a political field that was changing after decades of stability, but dynamism was always greatest at the top. Furthermore events within the political field were far removed from the protests that characterized the civic field since the 1950s. The interaction occurred only at a general level: since citizens saw environmental protection as a necessity of an affluent society, bureaucrats and politicians decided to do something.

All the time the third field of environmentalism, culture and life, was bleak. Some intellectuals continued to grumble about the profane materiality of modern life, but most people were happy to enjoy the pleasures of mass consumption. Some traditions from the Life Reform movement survived, and biodynamic farmers continued to do their thing, but they inspired few people beyond their distinct spheres. With a bit of polemic, one might argue that in the 1950s and 1960s, the key thing about appreciating nature was whether one could get there by car.

This picture changed surprisingly little during the 1960s. German historians have come to see that decade as one of dynamism and upheaval, culminating in the student rebellion of 1968.[31] However, environmental issues were strangely disconnected from these events, a situation that has not received much attention from environmental historians so far. Protests seized on other topics: reforms in education, the controversial State of Emergency Laws that the federal government pushed through parliament, the reign of the Shah in Iran, and the US war in Vietnam. At the most, we see some common ground in protests against gentrification and urban renewal, but these issues appear green mostly in retrospect.[32] When it came to the environment, signs of change were visible first and foremost in an international context.

Globalizing Environmentalism I: 1945 to 1973

Very little survived from the nascent transnational network that existed before 1914. In a time of international conflicts, communication across borders was naturally difficult, and contacts remained coincidental and sporadic. While there were some initiatives after 1918—for example, at the newly established League of Nations—they did not go further than nonbinding debates. To be sure, these debates mirrored transnational agreement that problems like whaling or oil pollution of the seas required global attention. However, it had become no less clear just how long the path to multinational solutions would be.[33] Collaboration developed best in bilateral exchanges, especially where a concrete, shared concern existed. When Germany had to relinquish North Schleswig to Denmark after World War I, Conwentz, with German thoroughness, sent a list of the nature reserves.[34]

This changed only slowly after World War II. Growing affluence stimulated interest in a clean environment across Europe, but activities were mostly national and regional in scope. However, some of the results were remarkable, with the most spectacular event of the 1950s occurring in London. For centuries, smog had plagued the British metropolis, but even a series of dramatic "killer smogs" in the late nineteenth century had not brought real change. However, when the city was beset by yet another smog episode in December 1952, everything was different. By evaluating mortality statistics, physicians determined that the smog had killed several thousand Londoners, and a committee under the chairmanship of Hugh Beaver, the head of the Guinness brewery, recommended drastic measures. The Clean Air Act of 1956 made London smog a faint memory within a few short years.[35]

This success attracted attention in Germany, which in itself was a new phenomenon: environmental problems were increasingly becoming an international issue.[36] The situation had still been different in the interwar period. When a weather inversion created a toxic concentration of pollutants in the Belgian Meuse Valley in 1930, killing several dozen residents, the doyen of German air pollution control, Wilhelm Liesegang, declared tersely that the event was of "no general significance."[37] But now the realization was taking hold that Western consumer societies were wrestling with similar challenges, and this imparted a new relevance to the problems of other countries. For example, the mercury poisoning in Minamata in Japan as well as air pollution-induced Yokkaichi asthma attracted worldwide attention: what would once have been seen as local problems were now perceived as warning signs of industrialization. On the periphery of the Western world, however, the attention declined precipitously. While an air pollution disaster that killed twenty in the American town of Donora, Pennsylvania, in 1948 was internationally noted, a similar event in Poza Rica in Mexico two years later, with a similar number of victims, drew scant attention even in the academic literature.

Global communication and national frames of reference were thus closely connected: the gaze into the wider world was firmly rooted in realities at home. Bernhard Grzimek, probably Germany's most important cultural export in the environmental sphere in the 1950s, provides a good case in point. His work on behalf of wildlife reserves in East Africa was internationally recognized, and his documentary *Serengeti darf nicht sterben* [Serengeti Must Not Die] won an Oscar in 1960. At the same time, his TV show *Ein Platz für Tiere* [A Place for Animals], which aired more than one hundred and seventy episodes between 1956 and Grzimek's death in 1987, remained focused entirely on a West German audience. His broadcasts were sedate in style but aggressive in substance: Grzimek fought against fur coats, environmental toxins, hormones in cattle farming, and hen battery cages, and his images were so disturbing that he sometimes advised parents who were watching with their children to turn off the television. But the issue was always an individual problem and not a comprehensive challenge for modern society. Once the show was over, viewers did not have to change their lives but merely wire a donation to the Zoological Society Frankfurt—the bank account number was a routine part of the closing credits. Thus the wide world of animals shrank to a German format: cozy, easy to understand, and suitable for the living room.[38]

The fate of the Japanese fishing boat "Lucky Dragon V," which found itself downwind from a nuclear test on the Bikini Atoll on March 1, 1954, became the peak of transnational environmentalism during the 1950s. Only a few years earlier this incident might have escaped international attention: the number of victims was small, and only one of them died after seven months. Now, however, fears about radiation and a nuclear war inspired a transnational protest movement. Linus Pauling, the Nobel Prize-winning chemist, estimated that 10,000 people had already died or fallen ill with leukemia as a result of atmospheric nuclear testing. In 1957, a conference with twenty-two scientists in the small Canadian town of Pugwash launched an international movement that received the Nobel Peace Prize in 1995. Ever since the contamination of the "Lucky Dragon"—a name that henceforth sounded like a bitter irony—radiation was an issue that moved countless people and made its way also into popular culture. In 1962, Stan Lee published the first issue of his comic strip featuring scientist Bruce Banner who, because of an overdose of gamma radiation, mutates into the raging Hulk when provoked to anger.[39]

To be sure, the 1950s were also a time of nuclear euphoria, when hopes for the "peaceful atom" ran across the political spectrum, and yet expectations and fears coexisted uneasily. Advocates of nuclear power were eager to stress the differences between military and civil uses, particularly in Germany, which had maintained an abortive nuclear research program during World War II. In 1957, eighteen atomic scientists went public with a "Göttingen Manifesto," which called on the German government to refrain from the development of nuclear weapons. At the same time, "peaceful" uses should be supported "by all means." The Göttingen Manifesto made headlines, as it was a spectacular sign of dissent by 1950s standards. It was also a clever research management strategy since funding for nuclear science would be easier to obtain without military involvement, and a remarkably successful act of whitewashing for a group with a Nazi past.[40] In any case, the myth of a clear line between civil and military uses lingered for decades. Germany ultimately refrained from a nuclear weapons program, though surely not for lack of trying.[41]

The Göttingen Manifesto had a whiff of nineteenth-century politics: notable intellectuals writing a pamphlet to stimulate thinking. Amazingly, a public outcry followed on its heels, though the manifesto was probably less important here than support from the social democratic party (SPD) and the trade unions. Their "Fight Nuclear Death" [*Kampf dem Atomtod*] campaign became enormously popular in 1958, but it had a flash-in-the-pan quality: the sponsors dropped the issue like a hot potato after a few months. The campaign eventually gained some kind of permanence in the transnational Easter March tradition that started in 1960. Moreover radioactive fallout ceased to be a major problem once the nuclear powers had agreed to ban atmospheric testing in 1963. Still the debate had long-term consequences, as the issue assembled people from different countries around a common cause. It was also the first rehearsal for the kind of apocalyptic rhetoric that would later become one of the defining features of environmentalism.[42]

International communication on environmental issues continued in the 1960s, when the United States increasingly moved toward the center of attention. Germans and others watched with interest while an ecological civil society emerged on the other side of the Atlantic and discussed expressions of discontent no less diligently than other aspects of US culture. For example, Vance Packard's books on consumption were translated with striking speed: *The Hidden Persuaders* and *The Waste Makers* appeared in German in 1958 [*Die geheimen Verführer*] and 1961 [*Die große Verschwendung*], only a year after the English originals.[43] Rachel Carson's *Silent Spring* was discussed in the Hamburg weekly *Die Zeit* already in September 1962, only weeks after excerpts were published in *The New Yorker*. Shortly thereafter, the political magazine *Der Spiegel* set aside five pages for Carson's findings and scoffed that America's chemical industry "began to pop tranquilizers" even before the publication of *Silent Spring*.[44] *Die Zeit*, too, made no secret of its sympathies. The article opened with the following matter-of-fact statement: "Pesticides and chemicals for fighting insects are poisoning our environment and can cause cancer!"[45]

The vigorous response had much to do with the fact that the "Fight Nuclear Death" campaign had sensitized the West German public to notions of global contamination. *Der Spiegel*, for example, used the comparison to highlight the dangers of pesticides: "The poisonous rain growing ever thicker resembles in every detail the sprinkling of the earth with the radioactive dust stirred up by nuclear explosions."[46] What emerged here was a new type of threat that would become characteristic of the ecological age. So far, pollution problems had always been local, most of them could be registered by the senses, and damage was visible within a brief period of time. By contrast, the new dangers had no geographic, temporal, and sensory boundaries. What had previously been primarily a problem of certain regions, like the Ruhr region, now seemed like a fundamental challenge to which every inhabitant of the Western world was invariably exposed.

This implied a tremendous expansion of the horizon, one that had been long overdue in many respects. After all, there were many dangerous substances that had been the source of concerns in earlier decades, but that had not provoked concrete measures. However, the new threat was about more than a broader range of issues: the new dangers were also more insidious than all previously known threats. The consequences of smoke and dust had been easy to perceive with the eyes and were thus at least visually under control. Even cholera, for all its horrors, had the advantage that if one contracted it, one would quickly gain clarity about one's fate. By contrast, one could ruminate endlessly on insidious poisoning, mutations, and cancer risks without arriving at a secure finding, and this injected a new anxiety into debates over pollution.[47] In the process, debates became more general and vague, losing the preciseness that pollution issues had had when they had centered on bad odors or property damage. As early as 1964, *Der Spiegel* noted about the dangers of DDT: "The weapon that humanity has devised for its campaign against pests now threatens to turn against it."[48]

The debate surrounding Rachel Carson's *Silent Spring* was indicative in another respect as well: it showed the dynamism of public debates and how they transformed the issues at stake. The controversy that broke immediately upon publication came to reduce Carson's book to a tirade against pesticides. President Kennedy commissioned a thorough study of her claims, while the chemical lobby mocked her evidence, and so all attention focused on DDT. Yet the book was really a more fundamental warning to heed the complex interconnectedness of ecological processes, and to intervene with caution. Pesticides were merely a showcase of human hubris: since 1956, the US Department of Agriculture had conducted large spraying campaigns in a vain attempt to stop the spread of fire ants, testimony, in Carson's view, of a fundamentally flawed mindset. *Silent Spring* was therefore a call to humility, which fit perfectly with the author's modest character, but this call was mostly lost in the power play over DDT.[49]

Interestingly enough, the Club of Rome suffered a similar fate with its 1972 publication *The Limits to Growth*, which it had commissioned from the MIT researcher Dennis Meadows. Here, too, the real issue was a certain way of thinking, namely the absurd belief in exponential growth rates. However, the study was received as a warning of resource depletion, and this reading was further reduced to oil after the first oil price shock in the fall of 1973 seemed to confirm the warnings. Yet Meadows and his team had not carried out any studies of their own on the available oil reserves—they had used information from the oil industry. Moreover the study made no secret about the limitations of its computer-generated forecasts, something that was not common in the heydays of cybernetics and futurology. The authors and the Club of Rome were not concerned with concrete forecasts, but rather with a critique of an idea of growth that had become second nature to many affluent citizens during the postwar economic boom.[50]

The Limits to Growth thus touched a raw nerve, and this made it a first-rate international event. Millions of copies were sold in more than thirty languages, and the title became a shibboleth for the turning point in the early 1970s: a time of endless possibilities gave way to a time of limits and crises. However, it is revealing that the study was not commissioned by a distinct environmental organization. Instead, the Club of Rome, founded in 1968 by the Italian industrialist Aurelio Peccei and the OECD director Alexander King, felt a responsibility to take on the totality of the world's problems and emphasized their interconnections; the distinguished multinational circle spoke of "the problématique." Members were handpicked and preferentially men, and they regarded themselves quite matter-of-factly as a global avant-garde. In this it resembled the profile of the World Wildlife Fund created in 1961, whose first president was the Dutch prince consort Bernhard; he was followed in 1976 by the long-time head of Royal Dutch Shell, John Loudon. Internationally, organizations were still firmly in the hand of dignitaries.[51]

In the United States, however, one could sense already in the 1960s that the change of environmentalism would lead to a radical transformation in the system of leagues and institutions as it had evolved since the turn of the century. The traditional groups were not made for social mobilization and aggressive lobbying, and they had even more of a problem with the colorful characters that were now increasingly moving into the environmental community. The transformation of the Sierra Club provides a revealing case study. Since John Muir's death in 1914, the club had led a fairly quiet existence for decades, until its executive director, David Brower, placed the struggle against dam projects at the center of the organization's work. A campaign against a reservoir lake in the Grand Canyon raised the national profile of the Sierra Club, led to a dramatic rise in membership, and eventually achieved the cancellation of the project. Internally, however, tensions with the charismatic Brower grew until he finally quit in 1969 to create a new organization under the name Friends of the Earth. A union with like-minded environmentalists in Great Britain, France, and Sweden in 1971 created Friends of the Earth International, the first international environmental organization with real grassroots members.[52]

Mobilization reached its first climax on April 22, 1970. The initiative of Wisconsin senator Gaylord Nelson to make this a day of environmental action achieved a response beyond the wildest hopes. Originally planned as a student teach-in, the event has gone down in American history under the name Earth Day. Millions of Americans took part in some 12,000 events all over the country, and activists drew on the experience and the post-event infrastructure for a long time, giving the US environmental movement a head start over other Western countries.[53] Earth Day showed the acclaim that environmental issues enjoyed at this time, though success was probably more than a matter of awareness: it also offered a welcome respite from divisive political issues to a politically active citizenry. It was no coincidence that environmental problems were booming at the very time when protests against the Vietnam War and the Civil Rights movement had passed their zeniths. While those issues had split American society, a celebration of the planet that all humans invariably shared promised at least a temporary reconciliation. Fittingly, Earth Day was planned and celebrated as a cross-party event involving all Americans.

Earth Day was a purely American event, though it became a global endeavor with the Earth Day celebrations of 1990. However, it overlapped with an initiative of the Council of Europe, which declared 1970 the European Conservation Year. Events during this year gave a heightened visibility to environmental issues, even though much of it, compared to the social dynamism of Earth Day, bore a rather official character. Furthermore the activism that many countries displayed within the framework of the European Conservation Year had much to do with the fact that in 1968 the General Assembly of the United Nations had decided to hold a large environmental conference in Stockholm in June 1972. Until the environmental summit in Rio de Janeiro in 1992, this conference was the largest of its kind. However, all in all, it was a fairly mixed experience.[54]

On the one hand, the presence of more than 1,200 delegates from 114 countries showed the growing political clout of ecological issues. On the other hand, Stockholm also revealed that the environmental debate was at that time an activity of the Western world, as the Global South took its own view of the new planetary awareness. "Are not poverty and need the greatest polluters?" India's Prime Minister Indira Gandhi asked at the environmental summit in Stockholm.[55] From the perspective of the developing countries, Western-style environmental protection was primarily a luxury, if not an outright neocolonial imposition that obstructed the Global South in the exercise of its right to development. But the conflict between the environment and development was only one of multiple dimensions of the North–South conflict that turned the global exchange on environmental issues into a rather complex discussion with multiple fronts. For example, among the horror scenarios that were passionately discussed around 1970 were also strands of neo-Malthusianism, with the American Paul Ehrlich and his book *The Population Bomb* receiving the most attention.[56] To be sure, the world's population was indeed increasing at a rapid pace from the middle of the century on, but this growth took place chiefly in the countries of the Global South. Those who discussed population growth in environmental circles thus came under suspicion of wanting to divert attention away from the West's overwhelming responsibility for resource depletion and environmental pollution.

The environmental summit in Stockholm was burdened not only by the North–South divide but also by the boycott of the Socialist countries. Ostensibly this had to do with a dispute over East Germany's status under international law, yet the move showed just how much Eastern Europe had disconnected itself from the developments of the West. Socialist countries mostly lacked the resources for effective measures against environmental problems, but they had plenty of means to suppress demands for more protection. Their penchant for large-scale projects with horrendous side effects did the rest; Stalin's

1948 Great Plan for the Transformation of Nature propelled the Soviet fascination with large technological systems into the realm of megalomania.[57] Three years later Stalin signed a decree that reduced the area under conservation protection by 90 percent—a dramatic measure that had no parallel in Western countries.[58] To be sure, it would be inadequate to write the environmental history of the Eastern Bloc as solely a history of catastrophes, especially since Socialist countries were sometimes having remarkably frank discussions about some environmental problems. However, Socialist Eastern Europe never developed an environmental philosophy that seriously challenged Western-style environmentalism.

On the background of these developments in Eastern Europe and the Global South, we can recognize more clearly the broad trend all over the West. In North America and Western Europe, we can find a heightened attention to ecological problems, a merger of previously isolated debates about the protection of animals and nature, resource use and pollution into one great "environmental discourse," a growing protest beyond established channels and critical reporting by the media—and all this culminated in a consensus that environmental issues were a key challenge for modern societies. Political responses came thick and fast in the run-up to Stockholm: Great Britain created a Royal Commission on Environmental Pollution and a Department of the Environment in 1970, that same year the United States created the Environmental Protection Agency, and in France in 1971 Robert Poujade became the first Minister of the Environment in a European country. That Poujade resigned only three years later and published his memoirs entitled *The Ministry of the Impossible* merely underscored the new status that environmental issues had acquired in the Western world. The environment was now serious business.[59]

This seriousness was probably the crucial new element that defined the time around 1970 as a watershed for modern environmentalism. We find surprisingly few problems or concepts that were truly new at this time. Even ecology, which rose to become the leitmotif of political rhetoric at that time, had a long tradition as a technical term in biology. What *was* new, however, was that it was no longer possible to smile indulgently at individual concerns and marginalize them. The issue was no longer just dangerous chemicals or endangered hamsters, but an all-encompassing environmental crisis that had many dimensions. As a result debates gained a new kind of urgency after 1970—a transformative moment that has stood the test of time. The issue was no longer merely a collection of disparate problems, but also one very large problem, indeed the greatest challenge of all: the survival of humankind and of the biosphere.

This new urgency was palpable throughout the Western world. But at the same time it did not imply a fundamental challenge to national autonomy. Quite the contrary: in the 1970s and early 1980s, environmental policy remained a matter that was still firmly in the hands of the nation-states. To be sure, the United Nations Environment Program, headquartered in Nairobi, came out of the Stockholm conference, and the European Economic Community presented its first environmental action program in the fall of 1973, but these were simply recommendations, which the member states could deal with pretty much as they saw fit. Even when these activities resulted in binding treaties under international law, the prescriptions remained very soft: for example, the Ramsar Convention of 1971, which 160 countries have now joined, obliged the signatories merely to report wetlands of international importance to UNESCO and to send regular updates on their status. Since plans for cross-border regulation remained illusory for the time being, there was much room for distinct developments in individual countries. Whereas a certain coordination of environmental debates was evident in the run-up to Stockholm, at least in the Western World, the trend after 1972 was merely toward a renationalization of these debates. While countries continued to talk with each other about environmental issues, they actually pursued paths that were shaped above all by the peculiarities of each country. The following chapter describes the West German path.

New Administrations, New Protests: German Environmentalism in the 1970s

The federal election in September 1969 brought a watershed in German political history. The Christian Democrats, which had ruled the Federal Republic since its inception, were voted out of government, and a new coalition of social democrats and liberals took over. The new Chancellor, Willy Brandt, won international acclaim for his *Ostpolitik*, which paved the way for détente during the 1970s. After landmark agreements with the Soviet Union and Poland, Brandt was awarded the Nobel Peace Prize in 1971. However, Brandt's diplomacy was just one facet of a broad reformist agenda that sought to make Germany more modern and democratic. Fittingly, environmental issues received a boost from the new government as well.

Environmental reform started in the most inconspicuous way, with the transfer of a division for noise abatement and air and water pollution control from the Health Ministry to the Ministry of the Interior. Transfers of this kind often have an air of horse-trading, and political tactics surely played a role, as the two ministries fell to different parties. However, the new Federal Minister of the Interior, Hans-Dietrich Genscher, seized the opportunity. His ambitions were evident already in the search for an alternative to the division's bulky name. On December 7, 1969, he decided on "Division U," and the letter stood for a previously unknown term: *Umweltschutz*. It was the literal translation of the English term "environmental

protection," and the word *Umweltschutz* was thus, as Jens Ivo
Engels has noted, "a bureaucratic creation par excellence."[60]
In 1971, Genscher presented the first environmental program
of a federal government, and he used the opportunity for a
programmatic speech. It was necessary to move "from environmental protection that responds merely on a case-by-case basis
to a comprehensive environmental policy," Genscher explained
to the *Bundestag*. He promised "to tackle the imminent environmental crisis at its root."[61]

The Division U pursued an ambitious reform program, one
that had no precedent in German environmental policy. A Law
against Airplane Noise and a Leaded Gasoline Act were passed
as early as 1971, followed by the Trash Removal Law and the
DDT Law (both 1972), the Federal Air Quality Act (1974), the
Federal Forest Act (1975), and the Federal Nature Protection
Act (1976). The emphasis lay on pollution control, the purpose
of no fewer than 34 of the total of 54 new laws and ordinances
by 1976.[62] Genscher also created the Expert Council for Environmental Questions [*Sachverständigenrat für Umweltfragen*] in 1971 and the Federal Department for the Environment
[*Umweltbundesamt*] in Berlin, which began its work in 1974.
Further innovations included environmental committees at the
cabinet and department head levels, a Conference of State Environmental Ministers in session since 1972, and the appoint-
ment of Bernhard Grzimek as Conservation Commissioner of
the federal government.[63]

The public received the new policy with a good deal of
sympathy, and the neologism *Umweltschutz* became a word
in everyday use. Criticism arose largely from party-political
and administrative rivalries. That was the case, for example,
with the SPD-led Ministry for Labor and Social Affairs in
North Rhine-Westphalia, which felt that Genscher's grandiose rhetoric lacked respect for the work that had already been
done.[64] Bavaria, traditionally the staunchest defender of state

prerogatives in Germany, saw the federal initiative as an un-welcome intrusion: a memorandum from the Bavarian State Ministry for Labor and Social Welfare spoke of "threats" from the Federal Ministry, which had "to be countered with the loudest resistance."[65] But it is revealing that Bavaria ultimately decided not to oppose the federal move and instead sought to outdo Genscher's initiative. At the end of 1970, Bavaria cre-ated the first State Ministry for the Environment in Germany.[66]

In the competition over who would strike the best pose in environmental policy, Genscher retained the upper hand. The situation looked somewhat different with respect to substance: rhetoric about a new era of environmental responsibility must not distract from an enormous degree of continuity. The Fed-eral Ministry was cautious in its approach where reforms were already under way. For example, the Federal Air Quality Act passed in 1974 was modeled entirely on a North Rhine-West-phalian law of 1962. Genscher was well advised to proceed cautiously, as the West German constitution required the fed-eral government to cooperate with the states. Since 1972, waste disposal, air pollution control, and noise abatement all fell un-der the principle of concurring legislation, which mandated ne-gotiations between the states and the federal government. Fur-thermore implementation of the new regulations usually rested with the states. Of course, this exacerbated the basic problem of a reform policy from the top down: the bureaucrats in the federal and state ministries had at best a vague idea about implementation on the ground. The reformers showed little interest in such problems, possibly due to a feeling that they otherwise could no longer keep bombarding subordinates with ever-new regulations. The new Expert Council on Environmen-tal Questions finally broke the silence: "By common consensus, administrations, but also the public prosecutor's offices and the criminal courts, have so far not taken the legal provisions of environmental protection law seriously enough," the Council wrote in an expert opinion of 1974. In some cases, official behavior bordered "almost on a refusal to enforce the law."[67]

The "implementation gap in environmental law" became a standard phrase. To be sure, implementation problems were certainly not unusual by international standards, but the lack of any discussion about the problem made the West German situation more difficult than necessary. In any case, the creation of transparency and public oversight of administrative conduct were not part of the environmental policy of the federal government, and this was not the only thing that we can criticize in retrospect.[68] Genscher shied away from conflict with the electric utilities by forgoing the installation of sulfur scrubbers. While the harmful effect of sulfur dioxide on plants was long beyond dispute, and the first pilot plants were ready to go in the early 1970s (the state of North Rhine-Westphalia having financially supported their development), the power of the large energy producers and the coal interests made it politically expedient to let the issue rest. Not until 1977 did the first commercial flue gas desulfurization plant become operational in Wilhelmshaven, and five years later only seven out of a total of ninety large power plants had these scrubbers. Genscher proceeded with similar restraint when it came to automobile emissions. He simply ignored the US trend toward exhaust filters, with the result that cars continued to pollute the German air while cars for export were equipped with catalytic converters. In both cases the conflict was merely postponed: in the ecological 1980s, car makers and power plant operators came under enormous pressure from ecological protests.

Probably the most momentous failure concerned the speed limit. The federal government reacted to the 1973 oil crisis with emergency measures that included a general speed limit of 100 km/h on the autobahns and 80 km/h on country roads. German automobilism would probably have taken a different turn if that prohibition had not been repealed soon after; a compromise from the Federal Transportation Ministry, which called for a limit of 120 km/h, failed in March 1974. In this context lobbyists coined the slogan "Free Driving for Free Citizens" [*Freie Fahrt für freie Bürger*], which ever since has turned reform efforts into a political gamble. In this way unrestricted driving on German autobahns became a national myth, and the price has been terrible accidents, horrendous emissions, and a trend toward heavy sedans that made high speeds possible in the first place.[69]

The speed limit debacle was illustrative of the general approach to environmental issues: the goal was government policy, rather than a comprehensive effort at social reform. The new federal government liked to talk about enhancing "quality of life," but this never evolved into something resembling a political compass.[70] For the time being, the American way of life remained the consumerist model; in fact the American way of life was probably less ambiguous in Germany than it was in contemporary American society. German consumer protection trailed US developments, and when the critique of consumption finally became popular in the early 1970s, that was mostly due to interest from the New Left. There is no German consumer advocate that could compare with Ralph Nader to this day, and it is quite revealing that Nader's *Unsafe at Any Speed* was never translated into German.[71]

Genscher also sought to co-opt civic leagues. In this he was driven not only by the desire to gain an ally for his environmental policy but also by a strategic calculus on the part of the liberal party (FDP), and specifically the FDP's left wing. "Environmental protection takes precedence over the pursuit of profit and personal gain," the Liberals had proclaimed in 1971 in their Freiburg Theses, the climax of leftist liberalism in the Federal Republic.[72] Moreover, in Peter Menke–Glückert, Genscher had made an unorthodox liberal the leading thinker of the Division U, though he soon became a thorn in the side of the FDP's pro-business wing.[73] In any case, both party politics and the reformers' strategic considerations pointed toward a close collaboration with environmental initiatives, and the ministry maintained close contacts to some key organizations. In 1972 the Federal Minister of the Interior even provided assistance in the founding of the Federation of Citizen Initiatives on the Environment [*Bundesverband Bürgerinitiativen Umweltschutz*, or BBU], the umbrella organization for mushrooming environmental initiatives.[74] However, the radicalization of the environmental scene dashed hopes for a lobby with close ties to the state; the first chairman of the BBU, Hans-Helmuth Wüstenhagen, also a member of the FDP, resigned in 1977 in response to massive pressure from leftist groups. The aggressive tone in books and the media, which culminated in gloomy doomsday scenarios, did the rest. In short, while the FDP continued to hold some political capital in environmental circles, a new sense of urgency thwarted hopes for an alliance already before the rise of the Green Party. Environmentalists wanted to let off steam for now, rather than fall right away into new political dependencies.

However, what shone through in the efforts of the Federal Ministry was a motivation that tends to be overlooked in accounts of German environmental policy: officials pursued their own interests when it came to environmental protection. Civic players were naturally eager to present the state as a dithering leviathan, one that was able to rouse itself to undertake certain measures only after vigorous protest. In reality, though, agile administrators recognized that an aggressive environmental policy would allow an expansion of competencies and budgets. We can see this motivation at work in efforts to curtail the maneuvering room within the bureaucracy. The Conservation Commissioners were particularly affected, as their traditional independence was now regarded as a threat. After all, a citizen holding an honorary office and subject to no directives could easily make himself into a tribune of the people and cause the administration a lot of trouble. As a result in North Rhine-Westphalia, for example, the Conservation Commissioners were abolished and replaced by State Administrative Boards [*Landschaftsbeiräte*] in 1975; in addition the government created a new State Agency for Ecology, Landscape Development, and Forestry Planning [*Landesanstalt für Ökologie, Landschaftsentwicklung und Forstplanung*].[75] These measures were not merely about strengthening scientific expertise but also about the fact that such agencies fit much better into administrative hierarchies than the traditional network of commissioners. Reform policy thus went hand in hand with the desire of the bureaucracy to retain control amid all the dynamism.

Environmental historians have given scant attention to how the reins were now tightened within the bureaucracy. They usually focus on civil society, where protest reached a new level in the 1970s. Industry and infrastructure projects now had to reckon with massive opposition. In Karlsruhe, a citizen initiative prevented the expansion of an oil refinery. In the Rhineland, local action groups teamed up with the city of Duisburg to derail an industrial complex of VEBA Chemie on the Rhine near Orsoy.[76] At Frankfurt airport, protest against a new runway was alive for more than a decade.[77] However, no issue stirred emotions as much as nuclear power, the ecological problem par excellence since the mid-1970s. In no other country did the nuclear issue become as decisive for environmentalism as in Germany.

The protest against a nuclear power plant in Wyhl in southern Baden became the signal event. To be sure, there already had been local protests, for example with the power plant projects in Gundremmingen and Würgassen.[78] It was in Wyhl, however, where the protest reached a new quality: winegrowers forged an alliance with citizens from the region and students from nearby Freiburg, and local concerns gave rise to fundamental

Campaign poster for a 1971 rally against a chemical industry complex on the Rhine near Duisburg. Note that it promised "beat, beer, and oompah music" for the event, which suggests that the organizers were counting on a rather diverse group of protesters. Picture Bundesarchiv.

Pamphlet from a citizen initiative (*Bürgerinitiative*) against a new runway at Frankfurt airport, Germany's largest. The runway was eventually built after a decade of vigorous protest. However, when the airport sought another expansion, protesters won a ban on nighttime flights that was upheld in court in 2012, thus fulfilling the secondary demand of this 1979 leaflet. Picture Bundesarchiv.

doubts about atomic energy: "No nuclear power plant in Wyhl or anywhere else," was the slogan. Protest was no longer about petitions and demonstrations: when construction began in February 1975, irate citizens climbed over the steel wire, occupied the site, and set up a "Friendship House," which was soon home to a "People's College [*Volkshochschule*] Wyhl Forest." A pirate radio station broadcast antinuclear information. The protest of Wyhl has long since become a national myth, one that embodies what makes a democracy: people come together across deep divides, fight for a common goal, and in the end they win.[79]

The myth of Wyhl drew strongly on the nonviolent nature of the protest. While the state acted quite roughly and without respect for the local mood, protesters remained peaceful. Elsewhere, protest was less benign, with the result that the antinuclear demonstrations not only grew in size but also became increasingly violent. Presumably Wyhl is remembered with such enthusiasm because the events in other places provided little cause for pride: the "battle of Brokdorf" was fought on November 13, 1976, the "battle of Grohnde" on March 19, 1977. Both sides boosted their arms: the police with helicopters and water cannons, the demonstrators with blowtorches for the construction fence, coordinated volleys of stones, command centers and motorcycle messengers, and even their own corps of medical students for the wounded. Baton-wielding policemen, tear gas, and helicopters buzzing over the heads of the demonstrators at low altitudes—these were indeed civil warlike scenes that were deeply disturbing to both sides.[80]

However, public protest was only one aspect of the antinuclear movement. It also included counter-expertise that pushed the nuclear lobby onto the defensive with remarkable speed. There was plenty of fodder for critique: exploding pipes, obstinate fuel rods, blackouts—the early years of nuclear power were full of frightening incidents. In 1973, Holger Strohm

Brokdorf:
Der
Polizeistaat
in Aktion

"Brokdorf—The Police State in Action," ca. 1976: Clashes between protesters and the police became a defining feature of antinuclear demonstrations. They were disturbing to all parties involved. Picture Bundesarchiv.

published a critical documentation of nuclear power plants under the title *Friedlich in die Katastrophe* [Peacefully into the Catastrophe], which expanded to more than 1,200 pages by 1981 and reached six-digit sales figures.[81] The critique of nuclear power received additional support from the conversion of prominent nuclear experts like Klaus Traube.[82] In short, antinuclear protest met with doubts within the nuclear community, where independent voices became more and more marginalized. As energy interests had invested billions into nuclear power, they were increasingly averse to critical thinking.[83]

In the spring of 1979, a hearing on the Gorleben project showed the power of antinuclear expertise. The Gorleben project was about a "nuclear waste-disposal center," which was to comprise a reprocessing plant, waste treatment, and a permanent disposal site, to be built in the far east of Lower Saxony close to the East German border. There had been local opposition ever since the government had announced the location in 1977. It merged with the national network of antinuclear groups, as critical experts realized that the nuclear complex was especially vulnerable on the issue of reprocessing, a procedure that was susceptible to accidents and contamination. While the hearing was underway, news broke about a serious accident at the Three Mile Island nuclear power station in Harrisburg, Pennsylvania, where experts feared for days that the reactor might explode. In the end, the state government gave up. In a landmark declaration, the prime minister of Lower Saxony, Ernst Albrecht, recommended that the project of a reprocessing plant "not be pursued further": it might be technically possible, but it was not "politically feasible."[84] Albrecht spoke more bluntly in a cabinet meeting: "I don't want a civil war in my state."[85]

The Gorleben hearing was the first real success of the antinuclear movement. Nuclear power plants were built in Grohnde, Brokdorf, and many other places, eventually making Germany the fourth largest provider of nuclear electricity in the world. Political elites stood by nuclear power throughout the 1970s, but revealingly, they never allowed a referendum on the issue. The experience of Austria may have played a role: in 1978, the Austrian people voted to abstain from nuclear energy, thus scuttling a completed nuclear power plant in Zwentendorf and canceling plans for a few more.[86] At the most, German nuclear protests achieved a delaying action that led to the cancellation of several projects, including Wyhl. It turned out that construction plans had run far ahead of demand, which gives German nuclear history an ironic twist: in a way, antinuclear protesters saved the German utilities from a huge waste of money. At any rate, antinuclear sentiments did not achieve a complete victory, and the issue remained on the agenda for decades. Even the Gorleben decision was only a partial success: the authorities built an intermediary storage site and drafted plans for a permanent storage, and Gorleben remained on the map of ecological protest. Still Albrecht's decision was a turning point, a shock for nuclear energy managers, and an important learning experience for their opponents: it was indeed possible to achieve something with words.

However, it was revealing that what was perhaps the most important measure in environmental policy in the late 1970s was an act of renunciation. The federal government's offensive in environmental policy had long been fading out, and with it the aegis of state administrations. Genscher had moved on to the Foreign Ministry in 1974, and left-wing terrorism came to absorb most of the attention in the Federal Ministry of the Interior.[87] As it was, Helmut Schmidt, as Chancellor, made no secret of his low opinion of the green issue: "Focus on the essential" was the leitmotif of his first policy speech. That this in no way included environmental problems became evident in June 1975, when the Chancellor, during a closed conference at Gymnich Castle, blasted an environmental policy that was getting out of hand. That surely reflected the growing weight of environmental issues: for the first time, conservation, previously a topic irrelevant to the national economy, was perceived as a brake on growth. At last environmental policy had become important enough to be attacked by the Chancellor. Yet this was, understandably enough, poor consolation for an environmental scene that was becoming increasingly disillusioned.

While environmental policy was at bay, there was continuity in the technical-administrative work behind the scenes. The expert circles that had been put in place in the 1950s continued their work, and the federal policies of the early 1970s were an obvious encouragement. This was also reflected in the fact that the first contours of a promising new field of engineering became visible: environmental technology. Beginning in the 1970s there emerged journals and regional associations to furnish experts with information and contacts. The federal government supported this trend when it created, in 1979, an environmental innovation program, which has been in place to this day.[88] However, the goings-on behind the scenes also included a new toughness on the part of industry, which increasingly adopted an obstructionist stance. In his memoirs, Genscher wrote that the negotiations over the leaded gas law had been "an object lesson about the intransigence of some industry lobbyists when it came to environmental policy."[89]

If we summarize the general situation toward the end of the 1970s, the general picture looks eminently inclusive. There were encouraging signs in all three fields of environmentalism, but it was no forgone conclusion that these trends would continue, let alone mutually support each other. We now know that a tremendous boom of green issues followed in the 1980s, but that surprised observers and activists alike. It is only in retrospect that we can pinpoint specific reasons for this remarkable turn of affairs. The Green Germany as we know it today is to a large extent a product of the 1980s, born out of conditions that were both transnational and peculiarly German. But then, identifying these conditions requires us to take a step back from the hustle and bustle of political events and reflect more deeply on the underlying causes that drove the rise of environmentalism. That is what the following chapter intends to do.

The issue of underlying causes is surprisingly unpopular in environmental history. Most studies prefer to focus on the drama at play in politics and civil society, as the rapid sequence of events makes for an exciting narrative almost by itself. In the end, the rise of environmentalism comes across as a strangely faceless process, devoid of interests, social stratification, and all the other things that usually provide the backbone of history. But then, environmentalism did not grow by itself, and neither was its rise predestined, nor was it irresistible. It grew out of specific constellations of actors, out of interests, and out of political conditions that deserve careful scrutiny.

The following chapter differs from the previous one not only in terms of focus but also in intellectual ambition. It is a tentative exploration into an underdeveloped field of study: the goal is to stimulate a discussion about underlying causes and to highlight the rich reservoir of approaches that we can take toward an explanation for the rise of environmentalism. Even more fundamentally, the following discussion intends to show how much we are missing when we continue to contend ourselves with descriptions and fail to tackle that bigger question overhanging the history of modern environmentalism: why?

Interim Remarks: Explaining the Rise of Environmentalism

The rise of environmentalism is one of those things that seem easy to explain—until one takes a closer look. From a distance everything looks plain: the stellar rise of environmentalism over the last half-century makes it tempting to view it as a general watershed. Given the tremendous change in mindsets and structures, there surely must have been some deeper forces at work. Narratives often draw on something resembling a Hegelian *Weltgeist* in action, of general laws of history that made the rise of the green cause irresistible. With a bit of polemic, one might speak of a "reverse tomato theory": nations evolve somewhat naturally, and at some stage, they invariably turn green until they are ripe for the picking.

I have taken issue with these readings from a political standpoint in the introduction. Teleologies about a predestined rise of the greens have come to ring hollow: in the new millennium, we are more uncertain than ever whether there will be a green happy ending of history. However, there is also a scholarly case against teleology: it makes the history of environmentalism much more clear-cut than it should be. Depicting the history of environmentalism as a grand awakening makes for a strangely diffuse narrative that is devoid of actors, interests, and turning points. Thus, for anyone reflecting on the underlying causes, it is imperative to treat the rise of environmentalism as an uncertain and perhaps even unlikely turn of events. We need to see the rise of environmentalism as a process fraught with paradoxes and unresolved tensions—which is probably synonymous with saying that we are dealing with history as it usually is.

We should also cease to see the rise of environmentalism as a process that occurred in a vacuum. If we look at environmentalism in a broader context, we come across all sorts of mysterious coincidences. Environmentalism thrived when the gap between the rich and the poor grew. It meant an additional task for postwar nation-states, already fraught with the challenge of maintaining elaborate welfare systems. Why did Western environmentalism grow in a cold war setting and languish in an age of globalization? And how do we combine the rise of green fantasies with the general decline of utopian thinking since the 1970s? It is probably a testament to disciplinary fragmentation that few environmental historians have pondered these questions, let alone provided convincing answers. The history of environmentalism is dearly in need of context, both for methodological and academic reasons. Environmental historians will have a hard time convincing other historians of the importance of their work if they show no interest in theirs.[1]

It helps clarify the general frame of the following remarks. There is broad agreement that the transformation of environmentalism occurred after World War II and that it accelerated notably around 1970. As we have seen, there were quite a number of older traditions, and they held particular strength in the German case, but that must not distract from the fundamental differences: since the 1970s, environmentalism had more public visibility, NGOs had more members, and environmental causes had more political clout than ever before. Any explanation should also keep in mind that the transformation of environmentalism occurred in all Western societies. However, there should be ample room as well for the peculiarities of German environmental history. As there is no uniform environmental-ism across the industrialized world, there probably should be no uniform explanation. Finally, the endeavor should keep an eye on all three fields of environmentalism. That, after all, was the peculiarity of the postwar years: each of these fields changed fundamentally, interacting with and reinforcing the others in a way that completely transformed politics, civil society, and culture and life.

We can dispense with two rather simplistic readings from the very beginning. One of them suggests that environmentalism emerged because problems cried for a solution. After all, many environmental problems existed already in the nineteenth century, and most of them remained unsolved for decades. Even more, there were quite a few signs of improvement after 1945. Life expectancy increased notably in the postwar years, and visible pollution was clearly on the decline by 1970. While the Santa Barbara oil spill and the Torrey Canyon disaster galvanized attention in the United States and Great Britain prior to 1970, there is no correlation between disasters and environmental activism in the German case. In the Central European context, the most spectacular industrial disaster of the seventies, the 1976 accident in a chemical factory in Seveso, Italy, occurred during a time of crisis for German environmentalism.[2] When the Chernobyl explosion and the disastrous Sandoz fire in Basel occurred in 1986, Germany's ecological 1980s were already in full swing.[3] In short, resorting to pressing problems is not only conceptually poor, it is also chronologically implausible.

It is no more convincing to see the transformation of environmentalism as the result of a few pivotal figures. Of course, the environmental movement had intellectual and political leaders, but they were merely riding a wave of discontent. It seems in fact that the environmental movement was more skeptical of charismatic figures than other social movements. In a number of countries we find the interesting phenomenon that environmentalists who received international acclaim were controversial in their home countries. Germany's best-known international environmentalist, Petra Kelly, was much despised and ridiculed among fellow activists and isolated within Germany's environmental community years before her violent death in 1992.[4] In France and Brazil, Jacques-Yves Cousteau and José Lutzenberger suffered similar fates.[5]

Among the approaches that deserve more in-depth discussion, Inglehart's theory of post-materialism has always exerted a particular charm on environmental historians.[6] In a nutshell, Inglehart argued that postwar societies experienced a transition from material to post-material values, which fundamentally transformed its social and political priorities. Inglehart spoke of a "silent revolution": whereas earlier generations had focused on things like secure housing and food, the post-materialists took these material conditions for granted and instead focused on self-realization and quality of life.[7] Inglehart's thesis became the linchpin of a huge transnational research enterprise, the World Values Survey, along with a revised version of modernization theory.[8] And yet the popularity of the Inglehart thesis probably rested on more than empirical and theoretical merits. After all, post-materialism casts environmentalists in a rather positive light. If environmentalism stemmed from a shift from materialist to post-materialist values, activists appeared as truly unselfish idealists.

It is hard to argue with Inglehart on a general level. It goes without saying that people who worry about their material existence have other priorities than people who don't. And yet as one moves from general observations to specific situations, the Inglehart thesis becomes notably diffuse. Post-materialism could sustain all sorts of causes, from peace to gay rights, making the argument aloof from historical context: it suggests a growing prominence of post-material concerns but gives no hint as to exactly which issues emerged when and how. Furthermore the interpretation suggests an exceedingly benign view of environmental protest in that it downplays personal interests. However, many environmental campaigns drew on the desperation of neighbors and citizens who had a lot to lose in material terms. Finally, it suggests a clarity of motivations that is probably unrealistic. If nuclear power or chemical pollutants instilled fear, was that a materialist or a post-materialist stance?

Environmental fears were often related to concerns about individual health, a topic that surely defies a dichotomy between material and post-material values. Popular perceptions about health and personal well-being were in fact so important that they provide a second explanation for the rise of environmentalism. The postwar years saw a momentous change in ideas about medicine and health. Contagious diseases and epidemics had lost most of their horrors since the late nineteenth century while cancer galvanized more attention. That implied a shift of focus from bacteria and viruses to hazardous substances, which made pollution a health issue of the first order. Furthermore the shift injected a disturbing element of uncertainty into reflections over personal health, as the causes of cancer and the effects of low-level poisoning are notoriously hard to define.[9]

The connection between environmentalism and health perceptions remains severely understudied, probably due to a notable distance between environmental history and medical history in Germany. It is quite revealing that more than half a century after the Thalidomide scandal that led to more than 2,000 newborns with severe birth defects, no historian has produced an authoritative book on the greatest pharmacological scandal of postwar Germany.[10] What we do know is that health concerns inspired a number of prominent environmentalists. Petra Kelly witnessed her sister dying from cancer as a

child, an experience that she shared in countless speeches. Bär-
bel Höhn, who served as minister for the environment in North
Rhine-Westphalia for ten years and is nowadays sitting in the
Bundestag, came to environmental issues when her son grew
sick from polluted air. We also know that alternative medicine
flourished on the heels of environmental sentiments, gaining
a prominence in German culture that it had not had since the
heydays of the Life Reform movement.

A third explanation highlights the changing economic context. Like most Western societies, Germany experienced a
gradual decline of industry and a boom in the service sector.
With that, a growing part of the population worked outside
the industrial sector, which obviously made it easier to criticize
polluters: the feeling was that the general population received
enormous burdens and no benefits from industry. Industrialists
found it hard to come up with a response, and some reactions
had an air of desperation. In 1983, employees of the chemical
giant Bayer founded an in-house citizen initiative to counter
attacks from environmental NGOs named *Malocher gegen
Schmarotzer* (which roughly translates as workers against free-
loaders—a name so embarrassing that they dropped it after
a few months).[11] In general, we can witness all over the West
a decline in the cultural hegemony of industry and a growing conviction that capitalists should not make profits at the
expense of the environment. The huge number of Green Party
members in civil service mirrors this detachment from the industrial sector quite nicely.[12]

The rise of environmentalism was also helped by concepts
such as ecology, and these concepts qualify as explanations in
their own right. Ecology enabled activists to connect different causes, and it surely made a difference whether an activist
joined a single-issue initiative or a broad environmental alliance. Networking was probably more effective than transfor-
mations in the issues: as we have seen, most environmental

concerns had long been legitimate issues before 1970. The media played a key role in this process, as they generally liked to talk about "the environmental movement" even when its members felt more comfortable as birdies or antinuclear campaigners. In any case, the broad roof called environmentalism was a crucial innovation that forever changed society's view of these issues. The infighting within the environmental camp remained mostly beyond the public radar.

Finally, one should also see the rise of environmentalism as a self-reinforcing process. In the 1970s and 1980s, environmentalism was amazingly successful all over the West, as laws and agencies were created by the dozen. That was all the more impressive for activists and the general population because there was another arena where solutions were hard to come by, and that was the economy. Historians have long recognized the early 1970s as a watershed: the growth rates of the miracle years disappeared, to be replaced by recession, unemployment, and rising public debt. The Bretton Woods system collapsed, and the 1973 oil crisis exposed the delicate resource base of Western affluent societies. Keynesian approaches lost credibility, neoliberal alternatives were controversial, and competition from East Asia looked ever more threatening.[13] By contrast, environmentalism offered commonsense solutions that could be achieved within a short period of time—a welcome respite from social and economic quandaries.

These five explanations pertain to Western societies in the late twentieth century generally. However, there were also a number of German peculiarities. For one, German environmentalism profoundly changed its political coloring. Traditionally nature protection and related efforts had tilted toward the political right, and that tradition was still alive in the 1970s. In 1975, a Christian Democratic politician, Herbert Gruhl, published a best-selling book with gloomy environmental predictions.[14] However, the left discovered the issue around that time, and environmentalism received a distinctly leftist imprint. The nuclear debate was the door opener, as it was particularly apt for Marxist interpretations. Terms like "nuclear fascism" or "*Atomstaat*," a word that alluded to the theory of state monopoly capitalism, reflected nothing short of a political takeover.[15]

To be sure, not every leftist made the transition from red to green. The youth division of the social democratic party mostly failed to catch the wave, thus creating a political vacuum that the Green Party filled with great success.[16] It was in fact quite an ideological feat to move from a Marxist vocabulary to an ecological one: after all, the exploitation of the proletariat was something rather different from the exploitation of nature.[17] However, dogmatic precision did not reign supreme for a left that had suffered a long string of defeats since the late 1960s. In a way, the left tried almost everything else to gain popularity, only to strike upon ecology at the very end.[18] The left's penchant for green causes always had an air of political opportunism. For an embattled left, ecology was tantamount to a last hope.

Amazingly, this act of rebranding drew little criticism from the political right. Only a few hardcore conservatives grew agitated and ruminated about ecology as a socialist Trojan horse.[19] New laws and agencies were approved with broad bipartisan support, a remarkable achievement given the huge number of political battles between both camps during the 1970s and 1980s. It helped that the left lost much of its political edge in the process. The Trojan horse was empty, so to speak: green issues did not bring Marxist theorems into the mainstream, except perhaps for a diffuse distrust of industry. After the 1970s, which Tony Judt has called "the most dispiriting decade of the twentieth century" in the life of the mind, it was good enough for a leftist that the masses were finally listening to them.[20] Why bother that they were revolting for the wrong reasons?

From the point of view of a German Marxist, going environmental meant becoming popular.[21]

The expansion of agencies and jurisdictions deserves some closer scrutiny, as it leads to another explanation that works particularly well in the German context. Few scholars have noted that the rise of environmental regulation was essentially anachronistic: it occurred at a time when states all over the West were facing limits. But what was paradoxical from the outside made environmental issues attractive for political insiders: in the 1970s and 1980s, ecology was one of the last causes that could justify a massive expansion of budgets and staff. We have seen that rationale at work in Genscher's policy initiative, and he was merely the first among a number of ambitious politicians who used opportunities to advance environmental regulation as well as their own careers: Joschka Fischer, Jo Leinen, Klaus Matthiesen, Monika Griefahn, Jochen Flasbarth, Fritz Vahrenholt, and Klaus Töpfer, to name just a few.[22] Farther down the hierarchy, many bureaucrats were thinking along similar lines, using environmental issues for their own vested interests. Political and administrative insiders received German activists and their causes with suspiciously open arms, and they made the environmentalists an offer that they couldn't refuse.

A third explanation departs from the observation that postwar Germany was a deeply insecure nation. The reasons are plain: Germany had lost two world wars and committed horrendous crimes against humanity. One scholar has even written a history of the Federal Republic as a constant quest for both internal and external security.[23] Since the 1970s, the crisis of the welfare state, the globalization of the world economy, and the erosion of state power have added to a sense of insecurity. Ecological risks implied another challenge to security, and yet they also had a countervailing effect. Environmentalism brought cognitive certainty, and a good dose of solace, too: in the middle of political, social, and economic upheaval, it was somewhat comforting to know that all these problems paled in comparison with the ecological crisis. The green patriotism that Germany has embraced so enthusiastically fits this interpretation nicely: for a country with a deeply disturbing history of nationalism, it was truly gratifying to find a type of collective identity that is actually safe.

Germany's sense of insecurity was also shaped by the cold war, which scholars are starting to explore in its significance for environmentalism. "The language of the cold war's global crisis and that of environmental crisis are strikingly similar," Jacob Hamblin noted in a recent book.[24] Germany was in a peculiar situation due to its location on the frontlines of the cold war. As a NATO member, Germany did not develop weapons of mass destruction, but it was their sure target: looking at a map of Europe, it was clear that Germany was the predestined battleground of World War III. The overlap between peace and environmental movements was particularly strong in Germany, and it seems that environmentalism drew a lot of its vigor from peace sentiments that could not go anywhere. After all, there was little that Germans could do with a view to the policies and strategies of the cold war powers. But maybe one could do something about the environment.

Finally, Germany eventually noticed that there was also an economic rationale. Put simply, many environmental problems called for technological solutions, and Germany was good at engineering. Green technology became an issue that united activists, researchers, and managers, creating perhaps the most enduring case for environmentalism. At times, the boosters of renewable energy sound uncomfortably reminiscent of the nuclear enthusiasts of the 1950s and 1960s, promising sustainable energy production, jobs for researchers and blue-collar workers, and a clean environment to boot. It seemed as if Germany had found the universal panacea, and it was painted in green.

All in all, this chapter identified nine driving forces behind the German environmental revolution. Needless to say, their significance varied over time: Marxist theorems had lost most of their force by the late 1980s while green engineering was taking off at that point. However, weighing individual causes against each other surely goes beyond the purposes of these exploratory remarks, and would actually be counterproductive in an endeavor that seeks to open doors. The goal here is merely to stimulate thinking among environmental historians and to move the field closer to the historiographic mainstream. If anything, the previous remarks confirm how deeply the rise of environmentalism was rooted in general history.

Finally, it is important to see that these explanations can only get us to a certain point. Germany had a number of good reasons to embrace environmental causes, perhaps more so than neighboring countries, and yet it helps to reiterate a point from the introduction: it is one thing to *have* environmental potential and quite another to actually *realize* it. Germany had been rather negligent in that respect, and few things qualified it as a particular eager advocate of environmentalism by the late 1970s. But that changed quite dramatically around 1980: an unexpected series of events transformed an average performer into the European vanguard of environmental causes. When scholars one day come up with a more sophisticated argument than the one I have offered here, chances are that they will add a tenth explanation: luck.

4

The Green Enigma: German Environmentalism, 1980 to 2013

Ecological 1980s: A West German *Sonderweg*

The early 1980s were crisis years all over the West. The second oil crisis of 1979/80 had shaken the economies of the West and triggered a severe depression. In the fall of 1982, almost one in ten Germans was unemployed, something unheard of since the miracle years. The crisis provoked strong reactions. The United States under Reagan and Great Britain under Thatcher opted for Neoliberalism, France under Mitterrand for social policy and nationalization, and the social-liberal coalition that had ruled West Germany since 1969 showed strains and finally broke apart in 1982. In this political setting, environmental problems were at best a political backwater and at worst a threat to freedom—Reagan's presidency began with an attack on what was allegedly out-of-control environmental regulation.[1] In the German context, Genscher's policy offensive had long since run out of steam and had yielded to a benign disinterest on the part of politics, and none of the established parties showed interest in a new environmental policy initiative. Even within the vanguard state of North Rhine-Westphalia, clean air ambitions ranked now behind concern over the future of coal mining. But out of this dreary situation arose a boom that has shaped German environmentalism, from NGOs and policy frameworks to ways of speaking and living, to this very day.

It is hard to understand this dramatic turn of affairs without the broad debate about "forest death" [*Waldsterben*] during the early 1980s. The issue hit a nerve, and soon politicians of every stripe professed their deep concern over the suffering forest: "When trees are at stake, we'll get a national movement," Hans-Jochen Vogel, the SPD candidate for the chancellorship, declared during the federal election campaign in 1983.[2] There is in fact much to suggest that one should see the forest death issue as "the decisive factor for the 'normalization' of conservation in West Germany."[3] The debate soon moved beyond woodlands, and forest death became a symbol for the ecological sins of industrialism. A motion of the Green Party proclaimed in May 1983: "Forest death represents a warning sign for an emerging, even greater ecological catastrophe."[4]

The threat of forest death brought a stagnant policy apparatus back to full speed. On July 1, 1983, an ordinance went into force that compelled power plant operators to build desulfurization plants within five years, and the installation of emission-cleansing catalytic converters became mandatory in cars. However, the quick pace suggests that the measures drew on previous work. Both measures had been the subjects of internal discussions for years, and only massive protest from industry had prevented them from moving forward. Strictly speaking, the fear of forest death had merely cleared a logjam, but an enthusiastic environmental movement showed little interest in such nuances. For them, forest death was proof positive that it was possible to force even large, powerful corporations to their knees with popular issues and zealous campaign work. Ever since, the belief in the power of the public campaign has been part of the genetic code of German environmentalism.[5]

The forest death debate boosted the electoral prospects of the Green Party. They captured 5.6 percent of the votes in the federal elections in March 1983 and thus entered parliament. The Greens were the first successful new party in Germany

"Can we still save Germany's environment?" Interestingly, that was a question publicized by the German federal government around 1982, mirroring the vigor of environmental sentiments. In the government's view, there was still ground for hope, "but we must all fight together." Picture Bundesarchiv.

since the 1950s, and their rise was all the more remarkable since their genesis looked more like an accident of history. Green and alternative lists had been competing on the ballot in various municipal elections since 1977. In 1978, green initiatives at state parliament elections achieved respectable results, but they remained below the 5 percent threshold. At the elections for the European parliament in 1979, as well, the entry into parliament was clearly missed with 3.2 percent of the votes. However, the informal Green Party Initiative received a reimbursement of 4.5 million marks for campaign expenses, and this created a powerful incentive for consolidation. In January 1980, at a turbulent founding congress in Karlsruhe, it was agreed to transform the temporary alliance into a formal party.[6]

The new party was basically an assembly point for divergent political currents. During its first months communists and conservatives sat side by side, until things got just a little too much for the latter; the attempt to set up a conservative ecological party mostly failed for lack of numbers.[7] However, even after the exodus of the conservative wing, the spectrum of opinions remained broad. There were eco-socialists and bourgeois ecologists, radical ecologists and eco-libertarians influenced by the Anthroposophy movement, urban alternative types and eco-farmers, feminists and gay activists, peaceniks and animal welfare activists, religious-spiritual currents and communist cadres. And then there was the issue of political alliances: while a *Realo* faction sought ties to the social democrats, a *Fundi* wing favored a more principled stance. The rift between *Realos* and *Fundis* remained visible into the twenty-first century, when coalitions were long part of political normalcy.

The Greens had quite a few hairy types, but also a remarkable number of celebrities. Petra Kelly, Rudolf Bahro, and Joschka Fischer were all charismatic in their own ways. Media figures like Hoimar von Ditfurth, the elder statesman of popular science in Germany, lent their prestige to the young bunch, and so did Joseph Beuys, one of the most influential artists in postwar Germany. The Green Party's Heinrich Böll Foundation is named after the 1972 Nobel Laureate in literature. All of that made for a colorful mix, and the diverse groups indulged in perennial conflicts over concepts and structures— they probably spent more time quarreling with each other than with rival parties at times. Only the specter of the 5 percent threshold kept the centrifugal forces in check.[8]

Changes were also underway in the network of associations within which traditional nature and homeland protection groups stood alongside agile environmental initiatives. In many cases the tensions over issues were at the same time generational conflicts: in the German League for Bird Protection, the clashes escalated so much that Jochen Flasbarth was on the verge of being fired as the chairman of the youth division.[9] In 1981, Greenpeace climbed its first German smokestack at the Hamburg chemical company Böhringer, thus establishing a new mode of civil disobedience aimed at maximum visibility in the media.[10] While one could not join Greenpeace, but only support the organization financially, the German League for Environment and Nature Protection followed the classic model of a member organization. However, some leagues failed to catch the wave: the German section of the World Union for the Protection of Life [*Weltbund zum Schutz des Lebens*], which had played an important role in the nuclear debates of the 1960s, developed into an extremist right-wing group. The international organization eventually expelled the German section in 1985.[11]

The ecological 1980s touched on many issues, some of which were sweeter than others. While pollution was a top concern, traditional nature protection waned in importance. For a group that had long been subject of international admiration, that was a change of tide, and certainly a consequential one. The new environmental movement cherished the icon of an endangered blue planet, and taking care of a specific nature reserve looked a bit old-fashioned by comparison—as if the various threats to the biosphere could somehow be kept out under a bell jar. In response, nature protection stuck to its traditional reliance on the power of the state, which caused many conflicts and eventually won this branch of environmentalism a reputation for legalism.[12] Except for a few charismatic species like whales, the protection of animals was also a backwater, possibly due to Bernhard Grzimek's cultural hegemony in this field: Grzimek's old-fashioned style certainly lacked the brash air of the ecological 1980s.[13] Whereas resources had been a key issue after the *Limits to Growth*, they received scant attention during the 1980s, probably a result of the collapse of the oil price in the middle of the decade.

All in all, the environmentalism of the 1980s favored catchier, visually attractive issues, and thankfully, there were still a few eye-catching problems around. In order to criticize the dumping of acid waste in the North Sea or the bloody hunt for whales, all that was needed were a few good images, which Greenpeace readily supplied. The chemical industry was under fire since a disastrous accident in Seveso, Italy, and the discussion continued when Egmont Koch and Fritz Vahrenholt published their 1978 book *Seveso ist überall* [Seveso Is Everywhere], an account on the "deadly risks of chemistry."[14] Together with nuclear power and genetic engineering, industrial chemistry became the epitome of "high-risk technologies" [*Risikotechnologie*]. The ozone hole stimulated another hot debate in the 1980s, though the problem had been subject to debates in the United States already in the mid-1970s. Beginning in 1986, Germans were concerned about climate change, courtesy of a legendary *Spiegel* cover that showed Cologne Cathedral halfway under water.[15] Thus, during the 1980s, we see the emergence of a canon of issues that has changed remarkably little since then.

This cover picture of 1986, with Cologne Cathedral drowning due to a rising sea level, marked the beginning of the debate over climate change in Germany.

The environmental toll of agriculture was another important issue, as farm production had changed dramatically in the previous decades. Since 1945 traditional farming had given way to industrial-style factory farming with grave environmental consequences, yet political reactions lagged for decades. In Genscher's environmental policy, agriculture had been a blind spot. It took the 1980s to put the issue on the agenda, a reflection of the broad, inclusive understanding of ecology during these years. However, as farming moved onto the agenda, the priorities of environmental policy mirrored the urban roots of environmentalism. Odor problems came first, particularly liquid manure, followed by nitrates, pesticides, and animal welfare. For farmers, ecological criticism always came from the outside: problems like erosion and soil compaction, which affected farmers more than consumers, ranged far down on the scale of priorities. The agro-environmental debate was always an imposition on farmers, a concern of people far removed from agriculture, and few attempts were made to construct environmental policy *with* the farmers. As a result environmental policy advanced much slower in agriculture than in many other areas. On the positive side, there was a boom of alternative agriculture since the 1980s, though organic farming still claims no more than five percent of the total land under cultivation today.[16]

Organic food found new outlets in the eco-stores that sprang up everywhere in the 1980s. After all, environmentalism was no longer about specific problems only, as it had been in the 1970s. It was now about lifestyles: environmental sentiments found an expression in new consumption patterns and styles of behavior. Not everyone took it as far as the chaps with long hair and full beards who now sat in the *Bundestag* and were stared at by some delegates like creatures from another planet. But some tributes to ecology were definitely fashionable: those who ate a vegetarian diet, wore Birkenstock sandals, or bought recycled paper were no longer weirdos. When it came to culture and life, nature had not possessed such a glowing attraction since the Life Reform movement at the turn of the century.

These repercussions in culture and life show how ecology brought diverse issues together. A narrow focus on individual problems gave way to an interconnected "ecological" thinking. The environment was thus also an intellectual challenge, and this contributed in no small measure to the charm of environmentalism. Individuals with a philosophical bent passionately debated alternatives to anthropocentrism or *The Imperative of Responsibility* as put forward by the late Hans Jonas.[17] Holistic thinkers from the turn of the century like Jakob von Uexküll and Rudolf Steiner became fashionable again. In the effusiveness of green feelings, people at times sailed close to the edge of contempt for humankind: in 1984 Carl Amery wrote that forest death was "the unmistakable attempt . . . of the Earth to rid itself of a failed species."[18] In a decade that strangely combined apocalyptic fears with computerism and technological euphoria, the greens represented the former strand.[19]

Many events mirrored and defined the rise of German environmentalism, but few were as significant as the explosion of reactor number 4 of the Chernobyl nuclear power plant in the early hours of April 26, 1986. The radioactive cloud first reached Sweden, where the operators of the Forsmark nuclear power plant initially suspected a leak in their own reactor because of the high radiation readings, and then Germany. The ensuing events confirmed what the antinuclear movement had been saying all along: nobody was prepared for a nuclear catastrophe. A cacophonous jumble of contradictory advice rained down upon a frightened citizenry that pondered a range of potentially momentous decisions. Could one still drink fresh milk? Should one stockpile canned goods? Were children still allowed to play outside? Or was it sufficient to fill sandboxes with new sand? There was no certainty except for the certainty of fear.[20]

In the wake of the Chernobyl disaster, the environmental discourse went into overdrive. Ulrich Beck's book *Risk Society*, penned before Chernobyl and published shortly thereafter, was enthusiastically received, as it seemed to encapsulate the feeling of the time.[21] Gudrun Pausewang wrote the youth novel *Die Wolke* [The Cloud] about a similar catastrophe at the nuclear power plant Grafenrheinfeld near Schweinfurt: published in 1987, it was in its twelfth printing by 1989, and is now mandatory reading at many schools.[22] The book was so grim that even the publisher got nervous. The guide for teachers cautioned, "The teacher must consider whether it is reasonable to allow younger students to read the 'Cloud' alone at home."[23]

The pro-nuclear federal government came under considerable pressure because of Chernobyl and tried zealously to polish its own ecological bona fides. The most visible sign was the creation of the Federal Ministry for the Environment, Nature Conservation, and Nuclear Safety in 1986, which finally brought environmentalism a cabinet seat. Following the brief tenure of Walter Wallmann, Klaus Töpfer made a name for himself as the second Federal Minister for the Environment with vigorous initiatives in environmental policy.[24] But Töpfer also avoided a rupture with existing regulatory traditions and pursued an evolutionary development of the institutional and legal setting through cautious, small measures. Since the 1950s, the motto "No experiments" had pervaded West Germany's environmental policy, and this did not change even in the ecological 1980s. Why wager on reforms with an uncertain outcome if insiders were recommending fine-tuning? As a result, even after the creation of the Ministry of the Environment, the federal government followed the motto that Peter Menke-Glückert of the Federal Ministry of the Interior had proclaimed in 1981: "The time of the large legislative endeavors is over—environmental policy is about implementation problems, finishing touches, improvements in administrative practice, cooperation with industry, the state of technology."[25]

After the Chernobyl disaster, antinuclear activists drew the sign for radioactivity on a lawn in downtown Munich. Picture Stadtarchiv München.

Reforms did meet with success, particularly in the field of pollution control, though it is a matter of debate whether that was due to clever law-making or to the new charisma of environmental issues. After all, the ecological 1980s bestowed environmental problems with a new importance in daily administrative routines. Since the nineteenth century, officials had attended to the pertinent problems for the most part in a fairly lackluster manner. The problems were often complicated, and there were few guidelines or model solutions. Pollution conflicts in particular were notorious within the halls of bureaucracy: the magnitude of the problem was usually difficult to determine, and often enough the conflict was merely part of a broader discord among neighbors. What had been merely a dreary object of dispute before 1970 was now, in the age of environmental policy, a core issue of modern societies, and this made for a new vigor in everyday administrative practice. Problems remained, but the aforementioned "implementation gap" shrunk enormously.

Achievements during the 1980s are even more impressive when one moves below the level of national politics. Cities traditionally held powerful roles in German politics, and they provided environmentalists with a distinct arena. One of the key reasons for the resilience of the Green Party lay in its strong performance in local politics, where environmental activists found an abundance of issues: traffic, garbage, energy, urban sanitation, green space. By challenging automobilism and consumerism, green issues were reinvigorating local politics while also defining the public image of environmentalism. It was local politics, far more than national debates over atomic energy and pollution, that showed how much environmentalism was about the quality of life.

Needless to say, the makers of environmental policy faced a lot of criticism, which for the most part demanded more aggressive action and a faster pace. Since 1982 the federal government had been in the hands of a center-right government of Christian Democrats and the liberal FDP under Chancellor Helmut Kohl, providing the leftist opposition with ample opportunities to vent its anger. And yet it was probably a fortunate coincidence that the environmentalists were not in power during the 1980s. Under the impression of widespread protests, the government tried to catch up with the new sentiment as best it could, thus making the center-right coalition far greener than it had intended to be.[26] As a result environmental problems became bipartisan issues, and the German right has been wary to embrace anti-ecological stances ever since.

In any case, the results of West Germany's environmental policy were certainly respectable by international standards. It was in fact the ecological 1980s that defined the international image of Germany in environmental circles: the Green Germany was born. As so often, it was a mixture of real achievements and pure chance. Green issues were truly booming in Germany during the 1980s—but the exceptional thing was that Germany had this boom when environmentalism was lagging in other countries. Timing was crucial: the ecological 1980s occurred right on the verge of a global boom of environmentalism. As environmentalists in other countries were searching for inspiration and support, Germany became the place to look.

The environmentalism of the 1980s preferred a pure green. Marxist interpretations from the 1970s were fading into the background: while the Green Party was certainly a leftist party, environmental issues were middle-of-the-road topics, open to numerous political factions. Interestingly, environmentalists of the left made few attempts to link green and social issues, and leading thinkers ostensibly played down the link: "poverty is hierarchic, smog is democratic," Ulrich Beck's *Risk Society* declared.[27] There was (and is) no German equivalent to the environmental justice movement in contemporary America, which makes it somewhat emblematic of European neglect in these matters. Characteristically, Bess' *Light-Green Society*, for all its merits, does not mention the depressed *banlieues* on the outskirts of major French cities.[28] Germany was not lacking environmental discrimination issues either. In 1985 investigative journalist Günter Wallraff published his best-selling book *Ganz Unten*, an eyewitness account of how Turkish workers lived in Germany, and while pollution figured prominently in the narrative, few readers took note.[29] With a view to the socioeconomic reality in Germany, the ecological 1980s always had a whiff of escapism.

However, the biggest problem was that regulation in the context of a nation-state had its limits, and these became ever more obvious during the ecological 1980s. The struggle against sulfur dioxide emissions from coal-fired power plants became

an international endeavor, and when it came to catalytic con-
verter in cars, practical reasons alone dictated a common approach within the European Community. Problems like the
ozone hole and global warming even required a global coordination of efforts. After the experience of the Stockholm
summit, the prospect of such cooperation surely looked dim.
However, the cold war subsided since the mid-1980s, dramatically improving the prospects of global environmental policy.
The scene was set for a brief but momentous heyday of global
environmentalism.

Globalizing Environmentalism II: The Green Ending of the Cold War

"The environment can be a bridge between the worlds of East
and West, and of North and South. . . . As a scientist, I salute
you: for with this agreement the worlds of science and public
affairs have taken a step closer together . . . a union which
must guide the affairs of the world into the next century."[30]
Mostafa Tolba, the Egyptian executive director of the United
Nations Environment Programme (UNEP), used big words
upon concluding the negotiations for the Montreal Protocol on
September 16, 1987. Twenty-five delegations had just signed a
treaty to protect the ozone layer—a treaty without precedent
in the history of international agreements. The signatory states
pledged to reduce the production of ozone-damaging substances by half within ten years, a goal that was scaled up at the
second treaty conference in London in 1990 to a production
stop by 2000. Never before had an international environmental agreement reached so deeply into the sovereignty of states.

Success was unexpected. In 1974, two US research teams
had proposed the hypothesis that sunlight broke up chlorofluorocarbons in the stratosphere and that the chlorine radicals
produced in the process could attack the ozone layer. In 1978,

these substances were prohibited as propellants in aerosol cans in the United States, but this left many other applications unchanged. A genuine solution demanded not only a ban on all essential uses of chlorofluorocarbons but also a coordinated international approach, and things initially did not look good. When an international working group of five countries formed in 1983 under the umbrella of the UNEP to begin negotiations, there were no countries from Eastern Europe or the Global South present. Three nonaligned states participated: Sweden, Finland, and Switzerland. The two other members, Canada and Norway, were not heavyweights in global affairs either. But when British scientists discovered an ozone hole above the Antarctic in 1985, negotiations picked up speed. With the Vienna Agreement of March 1985 to protect the ozone layer, the Montreal Protocol, and the tightening of the provisions in London, activists and policy brokers brought a multiyear negotiation process to a successful conclusion.

The Montreal Protocol was remarkable also because it cast a revealing spotlight on the ecological mood in West Germany. The ecological 1980s had been very intense, but also very German, with the result that the Federal Republic initially missed the development of international ozone diplomacy. Others assumed the leadership role: at the G7 summit in Venice in June 1987, it was President Reagan who brought about an agreement that elevated the protection of the ozone layer to the most urgent task of environmental policy.[31] In other ways, too, the German environmental community preferred to remain within the comfortable framework of the old Federal Republic. When the German League for Environment and Nature Protection (BUND) joined the international network Friends of the Earth in 1989 (thus becoming its first German partner organization after almost twenty years), the BUND's board noted remorsefully that its international work so far was "mostly based on chance."[32] To be sure, many German environmentalists called passionately for "global thinking," but in the end it amounted mostly to demands made upon other countries, formulated from a comfortable perch: Japanese whaling, French nuclear tests, Brazil's rainforest—for a while, it was amazingly simple to be a global environmentalist.

As in the early 1970s the United States became the pacesetter of global environmentalism. That mirrored a turnaround of Reagan's presidency, which had canceled its battle against the environmental movement after a few turbulent years. When America was baked by a heat wave in 1988, the expert discussion over global warming evolved into a broad public debate, driven by outspoken experts like James Hansen, who at a Senate hearing claimed "99 percent confidence" in proving global warming.[33] At the end of 1988, *Time Magazine* chose the endangered earth as the "planet of the year" instead of the "Man of the Year," and the new president, George Bush, appointed William Reilly as head of the Environmental Protection Agency, who had previously worked for two environmental organizations, the Conservation Foundation and the American section of the World Wildlife Fund.[34]

However, all this would not have led to a global boom in environmental issues if there had not also been considerable movement behind the Iron Curtain. The dissidents in Eastern Europe made the environment one of their central issues in the 1980s, in part out of tactical consideration but also in response to horrendous problems. One did not need any scientific measurements to notice the pollution of the environment by large industrial combines, such as the steelworks Nowa Huta near Cracow or Romania's Copșa Mică. After Chernobyl, discontent was voiced in the Soviet Union and elsewhere, as the disaster opened doors for a broader critique of the destruction of nature under Socialism.[35] In 1985, conservationists from Poland, Yugoslavia, Czechoslovakia, and Hungary joined to form the Greenway Network headquartered in Budapest. By 1989, it had also reached the other Socialist countries with the exception of Albania and Romania.[36]

Even before that, environmental issues had already provided something resembling an autonomous sphere under Socialist rule. The industrial development of Lake Baikal had triggered an intense controversy in the Soviet Union around 1960, which was even fought publicly in newspapers like *Komsomolskaya Pravda*.[37] However, in the 1980s the debate grew beyond specific issues, and after some hesitation, the Soviet leadership under Gorbachev was willing to join international agreements like the Montreal Protocol. Agreements to protect the environment were a convenient complement to the disarmament treaties. Moreover the topic had charisma. What could possibly demonstrate the end of cold war tensions better than humanity pulling together to save the planet?

The 1992 Earth Summit in Rio de Janeiro became the high point of the green euphoria. It found an enthusiastic echo around the world and has shaped the agenda of global environmental policy to this day. Three treaties came out of what was then the largest meeting of its kind: the Framework Convention on Climate Change, the Convention on Biological Diversity, and the Convention to Combat Desertification. However, the gulf between transnational enthusiasm and the nuts and bolts of international diplomacy became palpable already in Rio. It was one thing to proclaim in moving words the saving of the planet as the common task of humanity, but quite another to translate that into binding regulations of international law. In his memoirs, Hubert Weinzierl, a prominent German environmentalist and member of the delegation, recounts how much the horse-trading behind the scenes disgusted him: "The noble words that were spoken reduced themselves in the final phase to paying."[38]

On the whole, the heyday of global environmentalism had a lot to do with a certain vacuum. It fell within the few short years when international politics was no longer dominated by the East–West conflict and not yet dominated by the globalization of the world economy.[39] As a result the Earth Summit eventually became an unsecured promise, rather than the great turnaround that enthused environmentalists in Rio. Some twenty years later, there is no help denying that global environmental policy has lost momentum. The United Nations Framework Convention on Climate Change went into force in 1994, but it took until 1997 to negotiate precise commitments for individual countries. The result of these negotiations, the Kyoto Protocol, was weak, especially when measured against the extent of the overall challenge. Nonetheless, ratification dragged on for seven years and was not completed until 2005. Since the protocol included no specifications beyond the year 2012, negotiations have long since begun on a sequel, but hope for a tougher post-Kyoto treaty, or in fact any post-2012 treaty, were brutally crushed at the 2009 Copenhagen summit. Since the Durban summit of 2011, the new goal is to have a global climate accord by 2015, but it is not difficult to find skeptics years before the deadline.

Of course, global warming is a particularly intricate challenge. And yet it helps put things into perspective when we note that among the three Rio agreements, the Framework Convention on Climate Change is still doing best. The Convention on Biodiversity lacks an implementation mechanism to this day, and the fight against desertification is seriously underfunded when compared to climate change and biodiversity. While environmentalists were hopeful in 1992 that the nations of the world would come together to preserve the global commons, that hope nowadays sounds terribly naïve. Even more, nobody seems to know how a reinvigoration could come about. We do not even know whether US opposition to international commitments is really a significant drawback or merely a convenient excuse for other countries.

Fortunately, global environmentalism is more than environmental diplomacy. Over the last decades, environmentalists have worked more than ever in an international context. Transnational networks and joint projects have changed environmentalism to such an extent that German environmentalists nowadays look back on the ecological 1980s with a sense of nostalgia: the old Federal Republic had a certain coziness that is gone for all intents and purposes in an era of globalization. However, worldwide networks of activists and NGOs look somewhat bloodless unless backed up by powerful political structures, and those are evolving only slowly, if at all. Environmentalism has never been more global than in our time, and yet never have people been more disillusioned about global environmentalism.

Needless to say, global environmentalism is complicated, and surely not a topic that we can discuss exhaustively within the confines of this book. However, what we can say is that the state of global environmentalism adds to an eminently inconclusive situation. Environmentalism has surely come to stay, both nationally and internationally, but lacks any idea as to where it will go. An optimist may call that an open future. Others might speak of a cause in crisis.

GDR Traditions: Ephemeral Environmentalism

The unification of the two German states in 1990 brought about the merger of two different environmental movements. At first glance, it looked like a process of mutual rapprochement. The West German Greens merged with what was left of the East German dissident movement and adopted the name "Bündnis 90–The Green Party," a tribute to the Bündnis 90 group that had formed during the revolution in the GDR.

The German League for Bird Protection even took over the name of its East German partner and has been operating ever since as German Nature Protection League [*Naturschutzbund Deutschland*], which was supplemented in 1992 by the snappier acronym NABU. But these gestures barely concealed a development that the East German side often experienced as marginalization and humiliation. Environmental law, institutional patterns, and ways of behavior were exported to the East without much ado, for the most part without questions about the specific conditions of the former GDR even being asked.

However, the GDR was certainly not a country without environmental traditions. A recent survey needed 1,100 pages to lay out the environmental history of East Germany in all its diversity.[40] With the 1954 Law for the Preservation and Cultivation of Homeland Nature, the 1970 State Cultivation Act, and the creation of a Ministry for Environmental Protection and Water Management at the beginning of 1972, the GDR was ahead of the Federal Republic by a few years. One particularly noteworthy achievement was the "Landscape Diagnosis of the GDR": beginning in 1950, about ninety landscape architects and regional planners systematically scoured the country for damage from emissions and mining, disturbances in the hydrological balance, and areas threatened by erosion. There was no similar investigation in the Federal Republic. During the 1960s, the GDR used financial incentives in the fight against air pollution and land use expansion while the Federal Republic remained focused on traditional command and control regulation.[41]

Similar to the West, environmental problems, as political issues, cut across the established lines of conflicts. Dogmatists did claim that the exploitation of nature had been abolished under Socialism much the same as the exploitation of the proletariat had been, though this is best seen as quaint ideological gymnastics. At any rate, environmental problems could be discussed fairly openly in the GDR. As long as one moved within the framework of officially sanctioned bodies and organizations and cultivated a rhetoric that was compatible with the political system, one did not take any major risk. Just as in the West, a healthy environment was considered a desirable complement to modern society. In 1971 General Secretary Erich Honecker called for more attention to environmental protection in his speech at the VIII Party Congress of the Socialist Unity Party [*Sozialistische Einheitspartei Deutschlands*: SED], though Honecker's prime motivation was the upcoming Stockholm summit.[42] His interest proved short-lived, and the Ministry for Environmental Protection and Water Management lacked real power in the byzantine bureaucratic structures of the GDR.

In East Germany, the prospects of an aggressive environmental policy were more constrained than in the Federal Republic. This was due, first of all, to the notorious shortage of human and financial resources, which characterized life in East Germany in general. Second, the GDR's economic trajectory involved extraordinary ecological strains. In the wake of the 1973 oil price shock, East Germany banked increasingly on lignite coal as a domestic source of energy, consuming no less than 40 percent of global lignite production by 1990. As a result carbon dioxide emissions per capita were nearly twice what they were in West Germany in 1988. Lignite coal also entailed devastation of landscapes on a large scale and excessive pollution of the air with dust and sulfur dioxide.[43] Another gloomy chapter was the mining of uranium in Saxony and Thuringia, where the Soviet–German Wismut Company, with around 45,000 employees, behaved like a state within the state.[44] In agriculture, the creation of large production units and the forced separation of plant and animal production had disastrous consequences. Third, a comparison of the two

In 1972 Hans Reichelt (right), the GDR Minister for Environmental Protection and Water Management listens to landscape architect Karl Oberle (second from right, with hat) on how to restore an open cast mine to agricultural use. However, ambitious plans fell victim to the scarcity of funds. Picture Bundesarchiv.

Germanys shows that the absence of a civil society counterweight was a huge handicap for environmental protection. The conservationists organized in the Culture League of the GDR [*Kulturbund der DDR*] were never able to generate pressure comparable to West German environmental protests, though some groups, especially those on "urban ecology" [*Stadtökologie*], were remarkably active.

In addition to these drawbacks, there was also a knowledge problem that culminated in 1982 in a decree by the Council of Ministers, which declared that all important information about the state of the environment was a state secret. In retrospect, there is much to suggest that this decree marks the point when the SED leaders lost control over the environmental debate. For two years, presentations on environmental issues ceased almost entirely, since no one knew any longer which information could be mentioned at events. This situation was all the more precarious as Western television was reporting at this very time with an alarmist tone about forest death and other environmental problems, and members of the West German Greens were making contact with East German activists.[45] The decree of the Council of Ministers also hurt the new Society for Nature and the Environment [*Gesellschaft für Natur und Umwelt*] within the Cultural League of the GDR, which had been set up in 1980 as an assembly point for the environmentally minded in order to tether this milieu to Socialism. Finally, secrecy about environmental information revealed a bad conscience—and it did not take scientific measurements to realize that the use of lignite coal meant bad air.

Environmental issues henceforth exerted a particular charm on all those who stood at arm's length to SED rule. There were obvious problems with the environment, some of which even clashed with existing laws, and talking about these issues was less risky than criticism aimed at the privileges of party leaders or the Stasi, the infamous secret police. The Protestant Church played an important role, as it was the only institution in the GDR that was able to offer room for uncensored debates about ecological issues as well as an infrastructure, all the way to its own printing presses. An ecological mindset thus joined with a spirit of recalcitrance, and environmental work was a constant tightrope walk at the edge of illegality. Open provocations were avoided—it went without saying that the environmental initiatives were in favor of the development of Socialism—and the preferred method was targeted pinpricks to prevail upon the authorities to change their behavior or simply to annoy them. Nobody could know at this time how great the danger really was, since the helplessness of the SED state in dealing with the ecological protest became evident only after the fall of the Wall.

The state of the environment in East Germany became a topic in the West even before the events of 1989. The GDR's first eco-novel, *Flugasche* [Fly Ash], was published by a West German publishing house in 1981. Written by Monika Maron, the book talked about the dismal situation in the industrial town of Bitterfeld, which Maron dubbed "the dirtiest town in Europe."[46] On June 25, 1988, East German environmental activists taped video footage on the disastrous conditions in the region, correctly figuring that the police would be distracted on that day: the Soviet Union was playing in the European Soccer Championship Final that afternoon.[47] A West German TV station used the material to produce a documentary, creatively entitled *Bitteres aus Bitterfeld* [Bitter News from Bitterfeld].[48] For people in the Federal Republic, the town became the synonym of Socialist environmental devastation, perhaps even more so than for East Germans.

Conditions in the GDR required a grassroots approach to environmental mobilization. However, decentralized structures were clearly unsatisfactory in the long run, and when the Green-Ecological Network Ark [*Grün-ökologisches Netzwerk Arche*] began to bring scattered initiatives together, many groups were torn between chances and dangers. Before the foundation of the network, the Stasi had launched a raid against the environmental library at the East Berlin *Zionsgemeinde* in the night of November 25, 1987, which set off spontaneous fraternization among GDR environmentalists with vigils and other types of protest. The raid was a defeat for the state powers, as the Stasi found nothing strictly illegal, but the incident could stoke fears about even harsher moves. Those did not materialize, however, and eventually the Network Ark provided a platform in November 1989 for the creation of a Green Party in the GDR.[49]

As part of the dissident movement, the environmental scene in the GDR made a substantial contribution to bringing down the SED regime in 1989. After that, however, it turned out that the East German structures were quite at odds with the demands of an open society. The easiest step was breaking away from the structures of the Protestant Church, which was no longer needed for protection from an oppressive state. More difficult was dealing with the grassroots democratic structures, which constituted the soul, so to speak, of the environmental scene. The Green League [*Grüne Liga*], which formed during the months after the fall of the Wall as a gathering place for the scattered initiatives, regards itself to this day chiefly as a network of ecological groups, associations, and initiatives in the five East German states, which is why it finds itself mostly in the shadow of the more strongly centralized and media-savvy environmental groups of the West German type. Finally, the East German environmental scene could no longer limit itself to addressing demands and wishes to a deaf bureaucracy. East German environmentalists now had to come up with solutions and take responsibility for them, and do so within a new legal and institutional framework.

Under these conditions, was there an alternative to the dissolution of the East German tradition? The rapid pace of reunification made it hard to reflect on the overall challenge, let alone respond decisively. As it were, a rapid succession of four electoral campaigns over the course of 1990 meant, for all the democratic euphoria, an enormous workload. The GDR's remarkably efficient recycling system, which had grown out of the notorious shortage of raw materials, unglamorously went under in the consumption frenzy during the months of reunification. In the end the GDR's legacy was primarily material. The cleanup of contaminated sites took many years, and it cost billions.

The ecological balance sheet leaned quite unexpectedly in a positive direction at the very last moment: East Germany's Council of Ministers, at its final session, created five national parks, six biosphere reserves, and three nature parks, in this way placing more than 4 percent of the country under conservation at a single stroke.[50] Conservationists have devoted special care to these areas in the following years, thus turning them into showpieces of German nature protection.[51] It was also gratifying that large sections of the former death strip along the inner-German border were earmarked for conservation and have now become a popular attraction as part of the "European Green Belt." But at the same time, people and institutions faded away, and in the end hardly anything was left of the GDR's environmental tradition.

The fate of East Germany's environmental movement was characteristic of the way reunification took place. And yet, the East German environmental community was particularly unfortunate in that it encountered a West German environmental movement that possessed enormous self-confidence in the wake of the ecological 1980s. The West Germans were more practiced in dealing with the media and better networked with parties and officials. And, more crucially, they *felt* superior. Thus reunification casts a spotlight on a West German environmental scene that saw itself as the social avant-garde around 1990 and never understood reunification as an opportunity for self-examination. This state of mind became even more obvious when environmentalism lost steam during the following decade.

Sleepwalking through the 1990s

In the federal elections of December 2, 1990, the Green Party gained only 4.8 percent of the West German vote and thus failed to meet the 5 percent threshold. In their election campaign, the Greens had presented themselves as an ill-tempered alternative to the reunification euphoria. The Greens instead banked on climate change: "Everyone is talking about Germany. We are talking about the weather," a campaign slogan declared.[52] In the run-up to the election there were once more hot conflicts within the party, which culminated in some members switching to the post-Socialist PDS. Two weeks before the election, the Berlin Greens ended their coalition with the SPD after twenty months, thus underscoring the notorious fragility of red-green alliances. And, to make matters even worse, the Greens had successfully brought a suit before the Supreme Court against an election law that would have allowed them to enter parliament. Once again, the Green Party had shown its talent for shooting itself in the foot.[53]

Within the party, however, the defeat soon appeared as a salutary shock. The Green Party became more disciplined and more moderate, helped by the departure of some radical ecologists. Another red-green state government was in power in Lower Saxony since 1990, and it became the first to survive a full legislative period; other stable alliances followed in Hesse, Saxony-Anhalt, North Rhine-Westphalia, Schleswig-Holstein, and Hamburg. While there had still been grandiose dreams of a coming age of ecology in the 1980s, ambitions were now scaled down. New institutions and journals appeared in the environmental field, and green technology firms were an expanding branch of business. Two research institutes of international fame, the Wuppertal Institute for Climate, Environment, and Energy and the Potsdam Institute for Climate Impact Research, were founded in 1991 and 1992.

In the early 1990s, there was also significant support from the European Union. During the 1980s, European institutions had emerged as crucial agents on cross-border problems like acid rain, automobile exhaust, and the protection of the ozone layer.[54] The directive on environmental impact reviews in 1985 began a series of political initiatives that eventually made the European Commission the most important pacesetter of environmental policy in Europe. The Single European Act of 1987 explicitly granted the European Union authority on environmental matters, which meant that initiatives no longer had to be sold as trade policy. Whether nitrates or waste, biodiversity or bird protection, noise or fine particulates—soon there was hardly an issue on which Brussels did not define the key parameters. Since the 1990s, European directives have shaped the general direction of environmental policy as well as many details; in the 15th legislative session of the German parliament from 2002 to 2005, for example, more than 80 percent of the new environmental laws could be traced back to European initiatives.[55] It is quite possible that the density of European rules and regulations would nowadays prevent a single country from darting ahead in the way that Germany did a quarter-century ago.

At first glance, then, everything pointed toward continuity. And yet, gloominess became evident in many discussions of the 1990s. "Environmental Policy on the Defensive" was the 1994 title of a collection of essays published in the paperback series *Fischer alternative*, which had been launched in 1975 and—as if to confirm the diagnosis—was suspended shortly after the volume's publication.[56] Instead, a market for eco-skeptical books emerged, though the critics never attained a prominence comparable to the United States.[57] *Der Spiegel*, too, reacted to the changed zeitgeist: while it had stoked environmental sentiments in the 1980s with critical reporting, it now redirected its focus to the environmental community. In 1991, it ran a cover story that chastised Greenpeace as a "money machine."

The article asserted that Greenpeace's strategy of well-publicized civil disobedience had made Greenpeace into a relatively wealthy NGO, though its resources paled in comparison with those of their opponents, the large companies that grew increasingly sophisticated in dealing with their stunts. Four years later, *Der Spiegel* published another cover story that took aim at environmentalism more broadly, suggesting a worrisome trend "from environmental protection to eco-madness." In the journal's reading, the formerly honorable concerns were now the obsession of "do-gooders."[58]

The new tune had much to do with the economic crisis in the wake of reunification and the icy wind of globalization. Against this backdrop, ecological concerns were now seen as obstacles to economic growth, which inspired a whole host of laws and decrees to speed up bureaucratic procedures. "Deregulation" was the new leitmotif of environmental policy. That made it easy for environmentalists to regard the trend as yesterday's thinking: an obsession with growth and mobility, progress for its own sake, regulation as a notorious obstacle—it all sounded familiar. At any rate, the new situation of the environmental movement did not inspire a great deal of soul-searching. For the moment environmentalists opted for a toned-down rhetoric and hoped for better days.

Some achievements from the 1980s turned into empty rituals. Discussions over quite a few issues look as if they had been shock-frosted in the mid-1980s, leading people to perpetuate lines from a bygone era in a twenty-first-century context.[59] Since the forest death debate, the federal government publishes an annual status report on the health of Germany's woodland. It uses indicators that are dubious at best, provoking feverish debates in expert circles, but little of that critique is ever discussed in public, as environmentalists and journalists comment on the figures with the same alarmist statements year in and year out.[60] In the controversy over genetic engineering,

In 1995 the German weekly *Der Spiegel* shocked the environmental community with this cover: was environmentalism turning into "a crusade of moralists"?

the discourse over "high-risk technologies" has turned into a distraction, as it presumes an impending catastrophe while chronic changes are emerging as the real danger of genetically modified organisms.[61] The dispute over nuclear power continued with vigor, particularly after the first shipment of used fuel rods to the Gorleben storage facility in 1995. However, demonstrations in Gorleben and nearby communities distracted from the fact that the days of nuclear power in Germany were numbered ever since reactors in the GDR were hastily switched off in 1990. No producer of nuclear energy has shown an interest in new projects in Germany since the late 1980s, amounting to a tacit admission that the nuclear age would end when the last of the existing reactors shuts down.[62]

In the midst of this crisis, news broke that, on April 30, 1995, Greenpeace activists had occupied the oil platform Brent Spar to prevent its disposal in the North Atlantic. After three weeks Shell cleared the platform, but the activists seized it again two weeks later, and the media reported on unfolding events in the North Sea with growing enthusiasm. The public reacted vigorously. The end of May saw the first calls to boycott Shell gas stations, and soon everyone was on board: unions and churches, conservative politicians and businessmen. By the time Shell finally capitulated on June 20, Brent Spar had set off the largest consumer boycott in Germany's postwar history.[63] However, the success took on a bitter aftertaste. After the unexpected victory, Greenpeace immediately launched the next campaign against French nuclear tests in the South Pacific, which ended in a resounding defeat. Moreover it soon became clear that Greenpeace had operated with false numbers about oil pollution during the campaign; the group's explanation drowned in disastrous media reports. And wasn't the oil industry merely one of many causes behind the pollution of the North Sea? The occupation of Brent Spar had in fact originally been intended as a symbolic protest on the occasion of the Fourth International Conference on the Protection of the North Sea in Esbjerg, Denmark. However, in the course of frenzied reporting, the symbol became the real issue, and Greenpeace did not attempt to redirect a campaign that was getting out of control.[64]

The Brent Spar campaign thus documented a gulf between the goals of organizations, on the one hand, and the media and public debate, on the other, and this gulf became a growing problem for the environmental movement. This was also a challenge for the animal protection organization PETA (People for the Ethical Treatment of Animals), the German branch of which had been founded the year before the Brent Spar campaign. PETA had a fairly ambitious agenda with its battle for animal rights as well as vegetarian and vegan diets. However, PETA made its name in the news with celebrities and their commitment to animal protection, as part of which models, for example, allowed themselves to be photographed in the nude for the campaign "I'd rather go naked than wear furs"—occasionally supplemented by an extra portion of outrage when celebrities betrayed their ethical principles. Insiders of environmental policy were disaffected and criticized the cheap morals of these campaigns: "Instead of recognizing the priorities of a modern environmental policy, we are constantly listening to a diffuse green sound tape," complained Menke-Glückert in 1995.[65]

From this perspective, the crisis of the 1990s was far more than a minor stalemate. It mirrored a growing gap between the three fields of environmentalism. In the 1980s, trends in civil society, environmental policy, and culture and life had occurred

When Greenpeace activists climbed the smokestack of the Boehringer chemical company in Hamburg in 1981, their courage received widespread praise. However, when Greenpeace occupied the Brent Spar oil platform fourteen years later, things had become a bit more complicated. Picture copyright Wolfgang Hain/Greenpeace.

in a fairly synchronous manner, making for synergies between the three fields. In the 1990s, things fell apart: what was popular was of third-rate importance in environmental policy—and ambitious measures like a gas price of 5 Deutschmarks, which the Green Party demanded in the federal elections in 1998, triggered a storm of outrage. While ecological concerns continued to enjoy public support, environmental activists gained a reputation as grumpy spoilsports, and became a cheap target of comedians. Environmentalism was still popular, but the environmentalists were not.

A stagnant movement is bound to provoke radicals, and Germany had its share of neo-Luddites and back-to-nature freaks. And yet it seems that their public reception has by and large been more benign than that of their British and American counterparts. Earth First! was generating quite a stir in the United States and elsewhere since the 1980s, as did animal rights activists with raids on laboratories.[66] Germany was certainly familiar with direct action—raids on fields with genetically modified plants come to mind—but they did not lead to a rift within the movement. Revealingly, the expression "radical ecology" has no popular equivalent in the German language. It probably played a role that the violent battles over nuclear power in the 1970s and 1980s had instilled a feeling of remorse on both sides, and citizens and the police are nowadays adhering to some commonsense rules. As a result environmental demonstrations sometimes have the air of a cat-and-mouse game. Whenever a nuclear transport was bound for the Gorleben storage, NGOs set up courses for activists with information on how to stay safe during a police bust.

In any case, radicalism was a minor problem compared with the quagmires of mainstream environmentalism. It was the classic problem of a movement after a boom: after dramatic victories with certain tactics, it was hard to advance to the next stage. Many experts were writing clever concept papers, but they increasingly did so in a vacuum. This was no longer the 1980s, when an excited public longed for new fodder to satisfy its taste for ecology. To put things simply, while the 1980s had been long on enthusiasm and rather short on innovative policy ideas, it was now the other way round. Environmentalism was at bay during the 1990s, and that would show when the Green Party moved into the spotlight of national policy in 1998.

The Red-Green Coalition, the End of Nuclear Dreams, and a Can Deposit: 1998 to 2005

During the ecological 1980s, a national coalition of the Green Party and the social democrats was the dream of many environmentalists. Conventional wisdom held that such a coalition would allow for comprehensive environmental modernization; in the parlance of 1968, advocates spoke of the "red-green project." The coalition materialized under Chancellor Gerhard Schröder in 1998, but it somehow lacked magic from the beginning. Compared with the victory of Tony Blair and New Labour in Great Britain the previous year, the red-green coalition had an unglamorous start.[67] It soon got worse. Eventually a sense of disillusionment set in, and most people had stopped speaking about a red-green project when the coalition was voted out of office in 2005. Revealingly, the defunct project prompted few efforts at self-reflection: while the Green Party had provoked a flurry of studies in the 1980s, the defeat of the Schröder government came across as the end of just another government.

This situation is remarkable in a German context, and even more so in a European setting. It was not the first national government with a green party member; that distinction goes to Finland, in 1995. But theirs was a multiparty coalition with the green party as a minor partner that gained only one ministry, that of the environment. The German situation was different:

the Green Party won three of fourteen ministries, including the prestigious post of secretary of state that Joschka Fischer held to great international acclaim. With that, the red-green coalition bravely embarked on a joint endeavor to change government policies as well as the style of government. However, a number of trends had eroded the foundation on which the project was supposed to rest.

Perhaps most crucial, neither party committed itself fully to the endeavor. The social democrats had a traditionalist and a neoliberal wing, with Chancellor Schröder clearly favoring the latter.[68] The first year in government was full of talk about a "new political center" [*Neue Mitte*] and a "third way" à la Anthony Giddens.[69] Meanwhile, the Green Party was open to neoliberal policies in the economic and social sphere, but not when it came to its core issues: it strongly favored state-centered solutions on the environment. With that, there were some overlaps, but no common intellectual foundation that united the entire government.[70] Furthermore, after many years in the opposition, quite a few politicians found it hard to make the transition to a ruling party, and it took some time until the coalition became a well-oiled government machine. Before the election, the Green Party had drawn criticism for structures and mindsets at odds with the needs of modern governance.[71] However, the situation was probably even worse with the social democrats, whose party chairman, Oskar Lafontaine, threw in the towel after less than half a year. Resigning also as federal minister of finance, Lafontaine turned into the undead of German politics, a constant thorn in the side of all leftist politicians in power.

The fall of 1998 was surely not the best time to start a domestic reform project. Germany entered the Kosovo War as part of a NATO coalition in 1999, which almost terminated the coalition after just a few months: for Germany, it was the first involvement in military conflict since 1945. Germany also hosted the G8 summit in 1999 and held the rotating EU presidency for six months, two tasks that tend to consume government resources. In 2000, the Internet bubble burst, resulting in economic stagnation for years. After the terrorist attacks on September 11, 2001, the coalition grudgingly accepted military involvement in Afghanistan. Only when the Christian Democrats became embroiled in a party finance scandal did the red-green project win a few calm months.

The respite was brief, and the opposition resumed its relentless attacks. In a way, the opposition was probably the staunchest believer in the red-green project, constantly suggesting that the new government would lead Germany down a disastrous path. Some of its favorite talking points were more reminiscent of the 1960s and 1970s than of the new millennium. They repeatedly staged empty disputes over a supposed lack of patriotism or reenactments of long-forgotten conflicts; at one point, Joschka Fischer's past as a radical in the 1970s almost toppled the government.[72] Both the Christian Democrats and the neoliberal FDP refrained from soul-searching after their defeat in 1998, and both would pay dearly for that course. When both parties were back in power in 2009, it soon became clear that they had no program of their own.

Nonetheless, the red-green government realized a number of significant environmental initiatives. It introduced a tax on energy and used the proceeds to subsidize employment, a clever combination of market-based regulation and labor policy. It expanded political support and subsidies for renewable energies. In 2000, the government signed an agreement with the operators of nuclear power plants to limit the lifespan of German reactors to 32 years. When mad cow disease terrified German consumers in early 2001, a Green Party woman, Renate Künast, took over the department of agriculture and encouraged organic farming and environmental regulations. After decades of subsidies and preferential legislation, the farming community was in a state of shock for months.

And yet all this failed to ignite excitement in environmental circles. The deal on nuclear power even drew massive criticism from the antinuclear camp, which called for an immediate shutdown. Furthermore a lot of red-green initiatives were not all that new. For one, German utilities had been obliged to subsidize electricity from renewable sources since 1991. Eco-friendly taxation already existed in ten European countries when the red-green coalition came into power.[73] Industries had invested billions to curb emissions, the favorite topic of the 1970s and 1980s, rendering pollution a moot issue. And, in any case, what could national policies do when environmental threats from global warming to the extinction of species transcended national boundaries? In an age of globalization, it seemed as if the nation-state had mostly exhausted its means.

Except for reforming the tax code, the red-green coalition stuck to the familiar paths and instruments of environmental policy. One of the great debacles of red-green environmentalism, the can deposit, stemmed directly from the government's reluctance to embrace new approaches. Alone, cans are surely not the kind of environmental issue that makes heroes. Many countries have found ways to deal with what is obviously a rather wasteful type of resource use. However, the minister for the environment Jürgen Trittin stuck to the corporatist tradition of German regulation: rather than imposing solutions by government fiat, his approach centered on negotiations with all those affected by the rules.[74] However, these negotiations over throwaway cans got wound up in an endless series of hearings and half-baked decisions that ultimately made no one happy. *Der Spiegel* even featured a cover story on the can deposit as illustrative of corporatist stagnation in Germany.[75]

To be sure, corporatism did not fail generally. It in fact was the secret behind many achievements that have won Germany international acclaim. The much-touted "energy transition" [*Energiewende*] toward renewables is based to a great extent on corporatist alliances. Eco-friendly taxation drew support from environmental NGOs and trade unions alike. Thermal insulation of buildings received a boost when the government joined forces with the construction industry. Even the fact that Germany nowadays produces some 20 percent of its electricity from renewable sources has as much to do with civic initiatives as with government policies. It is important to understand that the boom of alternative energy sources has challenged the cartel of the big utilities. Many wind mills and solar panels are owned by farmers, small investors, and municipalities, down to the nationally acclaimed "Schönau electricity rebels"—a post-Chernobyl parents' initiative in a small Black Forest town that eventually took over the community's power grid and started to sell nuclear- and coal-free electricity nationwide.[76]

However, the energy transition has reached a stage where the side effects are becoming increasingly plain. The German National Academy of Sciences Leopoldina recently sounded the alarm about energy crops, thus challenging the bioenergy sector in the middle of a spectacular boom.[77] Dealing with this criticism will challenge corporatist structures as well as the eco-technological euphoria that has become a hallmark of German environmentalism since the 1980s. For all the conflicts that environmental issues provoked over the last decades, the one thing that all sides could agree on was green technology. That consensus rests on an alliance of environmentalists and engineers that served both sides: activists were delighted about sophisticated solutions, German high-tech firms occupied an expanding branch of technology with great international prospects, and politicians were delighted that German industrialism was not doomed. The enthusiasm for green technology firms was in fact so great that it framed the German stance on international agreements. Whenever Germany pushed for strong commitments, there was usually a notion in the air that this would boost markets for technology made in Germany.

While other countries worry that excessive regulation may kill jobs, Germans are firmly convinced that "environmentalism creates jobs," at least in German engineering.[78]

Interestingly, green technology emerged as a distinct sector, rather than a theme that runs through the entire economy. We can see that in the German automobile industry, where ecology never became a defining issue. German cars remain heavy and fast, high on horsepower and poor when it comes to miles per gallon. When fine particulates became a hot issue in 2005, a stunned German public noticed that the French automobile industry set the industry standard for control. The automobile industry had political clout, most prominently in Chancellor Schröder, who touted himself as *Auto-Kanzler* after having served on the board of Volkswagen for a number of years. In a move that made headlines, Schröder forced his minister for the environment to veto an EU directive on dismantling and recycling of old vehicles. It was a spectacular nod to what is probably Europe's most impressive industrial complex, and industrialists did not fail to notice. Why should the government be tough on industry when it left the carmakers off the hook?

In 2002 Schröder narrowly won the federal election. Welfare reform came to dominate his second term, a topic that put the social democrats into the spotlight. Meanwhile, environmental issues were on the backburner; it almost seemed as if the environmental reform impulse had exhausted itself during the first four years. In the final days of the coalition, Schröder was ranting behind closed doors about excessive environmental regulation, but that probably says more about the way in which the red-green coalition was ending; after all, a penchant for negotiations and consensus seeking had run through the coalition's environmental policy. The red-green project did not conclude gracefully, as it crumbled during the final months and lay in pieces already on election day.[79]

The unglamorous end did not do justice to the coalition's record, as it clearly left its mark in German history. At the end of seven turbulent years, Germany was a different country: more diverse, more open to change, and certainly greener. In fact, most of the environmental legislation survives to this day, though one may speculate whether that was due to real convictions or the vagaries of politics. The 2005 federal election resulted in an unbeloved grand coalition of Christian Democrats and the social democrats. The environmental ministry fell into the latter's hand, and the incumbent, Sigmar Gabriel, preserved the legacy of the red-green years as best he could. When the social democrats left the federal government in 2009, eco-friendly taxation and other red-green reforms had become uncontroversial. German environmentalism had truly come a long way from the political hotbed of the 1970s and 1980s.

German Environmentalism after Fukushima

On June 30, 2011, the German parliament put an end to nuclear power. Of 600 members of parliament who cast a vote, 513 supported the bill of the government, the first nuclear law in a generation to win broad support across the political spectrum.[80] The law specified that eight reactors would shut down immediately and that the remaining nine units would need safety checks and go offline until 2022. At the same time, the government pledged to promote renewable energies. Two years after Fukushima, the decision stands out internationally as by far the most vigorous response to the nuclear disaster in Japan.

On first glance, the decision supports the contention that Germany is doing well when it comes to the environment. However, the real story is more ambiguous. For all the post-Fukushima pledges, it was also a clever political move for Chancellor Merkel, who had run a fragile center-right government since 2009. By getting rid of the divisive issue of nuclear power, she increased her options for future coalitions. The federal election campaign of 2013 was full of speculation about a potential alliance between greens and Christian Democrats. Merkel had in fact increased the lifespan of Germany's nuclear reactors just a few months before Fukushima, a decision that had provoked massive protest from the antinuclear camp. The new nuclear consensus was the result of a dramatic reversal, and it may be that yet another turnaround is currently in the making. When this book was finalized in the spring of 2013, much of the energy transition was effectively stalled due to growing concerns about costs and conflicts between the ministries of commerce and the environment.

The energy transition played a prominent role in the federal election of 2013, though in a surprisingly negative way. People from the government spent a great deal of time badmouthing the project, as if they were oblivious of the fact that they had started it in the first place. Even more astounding, politicians in charge offered little in the way of blueprints or policy initiatives to get the energy transition back on track, instead lamenting about rising costs for consumers. And then there were reports about technological blunders: while the election campaign was gathering steam, a diesel generator was churning on a platform in the North Sea to power an offshore windfarm so as to prevent the equipment from getting rusty because delays on the link to the offshore power grid have kept the otherwise finished project offline. For a country that takes pride in both engineering and organization, that is disturbing news.

The energy transition is emerging as a test case for political leadership in the twenty-first century. It is little exaggeration to say that in the two years since Merkel's bold proclamation, the government has mostly taken the hands off the steering wheel. Instead of comprehensive management, it has focused on generous subsidies, thus aggravating concerns over costs. But then, it would pay off politically to take a long view and lead a project for a generation in the age of the sound bite, when politicians think in terms of weeks and months at best? We must not forget that large infrastructure projects used to be run by powerful political leaders who stayed on the job for many years and staked their career on successful management. A new generation of builders, sensitive to environmental and community concerns and yet able to get things done, is nowhere in sight.

Angela Merkel won the federal election on September 22, 2013, though she needs a coalition partner to form a stable government; talks were still underway when this volume went to press. The energy transition is thus under negotiation, but some things can be taken for granted. There is no way that Germany will return to nuclear power in the foreseeable future. It is also rather certain that renewable energy will increase in significance. With 8.4 percent of the popular vote in the federal election and 63 seats in Parliament, the Green Party remains a major political force, and environmental NGOs retain great influence in politics and society. Consumers are paying attention to eco-logos and buy organic food in droves, and yet the future of the Green Germany looks more uncertain than ever. In a positive scenario, we are currently standing on the verge of another ecological boom. In a less positive one, we look forward to lackluster efforts to live up to grand environmental goals. Either way, we cannot conclude this book in a classic way, with a list of victories and lessons learned. The best guess is that the state of environmentalism in Germany is unstable, open to multiple futures that we can recognize in broad outlines only. In the end, Germany may be rather typical in that respect. Here and elsewhere, we are currently witnessing an environmentalism in mid passage.

5

German Environmentalism in Mid Passage

Every year millions of visitors come to Cologne to visit the famous cathedral. With some 10,000 square meters of windows and the tallest twin church towers in the world, it is by all means an impressive building. It is also a mirror of German history. Construction started in the thirteenth century, when the Gothic style was reigning supreme. In 1530, an imposing choir and parts of the south tower were standing when construction came to a halt during the Reformation. The project lay dormant for more than three centuries until German nationalists revived it in the nineteenth century. Having occupied the Rhineland in 1815, the Prussian monarchy embraced the project in order to improve relations with the catholic populace. Construction became a national endeavor, and thanks to a huge fundraising effort and support from the king's coffers, Cologne Cathedral was finally completed in 1880. Since then, it has stood as a joint monument to Catholicism, Prussian glory, and the German nation.[1]

Given its iconic character, it is not surprising that Cologne Cathedral has also played a role in environmental history. Since a landmark publication in 1907, damage from acid rain has been an enduring concern.[2] When *Der Spiegel* published a long article that was crucial for the forest death debate in 1981, it showed a defaced stone figure from the cathedral to highlight the impending danger.[3] Five years later, the magazine helped boost awareness of global warming with the aforementioned picture of the cathedral halfway under water.[4] More recently, the press boasted about wind turbines "as high as Cologne Cathedral."[5]

German environmentalism and Cologne Cathedral share a similar fate as international icons. Both make for remarkable edifices and have won great acclaim far and wide. And in both cases, the edifice looks the most impressive when seen from a distance. On second glance, one notices the scaffolding, the retrofits, and the dirt: it turns out the monument is not quite so monumental when seen up close. Cologne Cathedral has been a repair job since its inauguration, and a finished building is as elusive as a definitive version of German environmentalism. At the moment, some 60 artisans are working permanently on and around Cologne Cathedral.

As we have seen, German environmentalism is currently undergoing another renovation, and arguably a rather significant one. Ongoing changes touch on the basic frame of German environmentalism, the nation-state that has served as the political arena for more than a century and now faces the challenge of globalization: whatever we can say about the future of environmentalism, it will almost surely be more international. Therefore it would be misleading to conclude this book in a fashion that would presume a false level of maturity. At the moment, the most interesting thing about German environmentalism is not what it has achieved. The most interesting thing is that it is changing.

These concluding remarks are thus more akin to a visit of an active construction site. They look at the places where action is currently the most spectacular, and most revealing as to the overall direction of environmentalism. Needless to say, such an endeavor includes a good dose of subjective judgment as to where the key challenges lie. Some issues, such as the globalization of environmentalism, are subject to hot debates; some, such as the corporatist entanglement of German NGOs, are rather calm but probably shouldn't be. Yet all these challenges escape a quick fix: there is no easy solution in sight, or at least none that I would feel comfortable recommending. At the moment it seems best to aim for a precise description of where the problem lies, and some thoughts on where to look in the search for answers.

The transformation of environmentalism is an international and ultimately global process, and many societies, particularly those in the West, are currently facing challenges quite similar to those in the country under discussion here. Chances are that Germany does offer a particularly rewarding opportunity to discuss the ongoing transformation of environmentalism. It has solved a number of problems that other countries are still facing, making it more apt to confront new challenges. As it stands, German environmentalism has shown resilience to change, not least due to a strong dose of patriotic pride. Indeed, the stage is set for a clash between the old and the new, and the results may provide some hint as to whether we are currently witnessing the emergence of a new environmentalism. Germany may prove to be a laboratory for things to come.

Beyond the Obituaries

Times of change typically produce a distinct type of nervousness as stakeholders try to assess what ongoing trends may mean for them. However, for all the dynamism that we are witnessing, there is probably one thing that we can take for granted: for the foreseeable future, Germany will remain a green country. Environmental concerns continue to be popular, leading NGOs like the BUND and the NABU claim almost half a million members, and politicians seem loath to launch a Bush-style assault on environmental regulation. In Germany, environmentalism has come to stay.

That situation is remarkable in more than one respect. The history of German environmentalism is littered with warnings that the wave of environmental sentiments would soon fade out. The Green Party, in particular, has witnessed countless obituaries read for itself, in all types of sentiments: grateful, disillusioned, renegade. We have heard fewer of these voices in recent years, as the movement has shown remarkable resilience in the face of these declarations, and when the Green Party celebrated its thirtieth birthday in 2010, most observers described it as part of the political establishment. Environmentalism is, as Christopher Rootes has noted, "the great survivor among the new social movements that arose in and since the 1960s."[6]

With that, one of the major problems for German environmentalism may be complacency. Few Germans have heard about Ted Nordhaus and Michael Shellenberger and their provocative argument of an impending "death of environmentalism," let alone thought about it with a view to their own situation.[7] To be sure, change is happening, simply without much of a debate within or beyond environmental circles, and it is a bit of a mystery why this is the case. Intellectual stimulation was surely among the things that made environmentalism attractive in the 1970s and 1980s, and there is still plenty of fodder for an open-minded debate. German environmentalists may soon learn that there is a fine line between resilience and stagnation.

Beyond the Political Sphere

Among the three realms of German environmentalism, it was the political field that attracted the most attention internationally. Other countries had more powerful NGOs and tastier organic food, but when it came to politics, the dramatic gains during the 1980s were without parallel across the West. No other country got rid of sulfur emissions from coal-fired power plants within five years, and when it came to environmental regulation within the European Union, one could usually trust in Germany as an ally. At its core, the boom in environmental policy stemmed from a perfect division of labor between civil society and the state. Irate citizens pointed to issues and called for abatement—the state solved the problems. For a while, German environmental policy was riding a wave of success.

But at some point, Germany began running out of problems that matched that approach. Everything was easy as long as pollution was the defining issue: if the modern state was able to do anything, it was surely to discipline and punish polluters. Nowadays many environmental challenges defy prosecution and punishment. Even more, the penchant for bans and controls has backfired and provided environmentalism with an air of negativity. A movement that puts laws and restrictions center stage does not look all that attractive in the twenty-first century.

While legal limits will likely remain important for many environmental issues, it is crucial that environmentalism move beyond politics. The range of remaining issues seem to defy a political fix: they stem from certain ways of life. What can the state do when its citizens buy big SUVs, choose a long commute to work, and fly to Mediterranean beaches five times a year? None of this is illegal, but can add up to an obscene environmental toll.

The lingering crisis of the global economy provides a good opportunity to start a new discussion about lifestyles and the environment. Since the 1970s, calls for moderation and self-restraint have fallen on deaf ears in a society obsessed with growth, as the controversial debate over the Club of Rome's *Limits to Growth* serves to attest. However, growth has lost the air of a self-evident goal, to be supplanted by a nagging uncertainty about the future of Western consumer societies. With that, the notion of limits to growth is no longer all that provocative. We all know that they exist.[8]

Of course, debates over lifestyles have their own challenges. Environmental concerns can easily become caught in a whirl-wind of short-lived fashions. For example, are people who seek a "lifestyle of health and sustainability" (colloquially called LOHAS) more than an ephemeral phenomenon? However, the endeavor also offers tremendous opportunities. Debates over lifestyles can give environmentalism a positive, creative image. For a movement that has come to be associated with billowing smokestacks and dying whales, that could mean a momentous about-face. The new environmentalism could actually be fun.

An engagement with lifestyle issues will almost surely make environmentalism more colorful and thematically diverse. It can also open new lines of communication. For instance, it opens the door for a talk with religions, including non-Christian

Volkswagen car advertising Rapunzel organic food in Tübingen, ca. 2005. Lifestyles will be a key issue for environmentalism in the twenty-first century, and not just in this counterculture version. Picture Björn Appel.

ones. Wouldn't it be great if we could bring the hugely contentious debate over Islam in Germany into the environmental arena? Urban gardening is another topic where environmentalism and lifestyles merge in a most promising way. In any case, the key is to present environmentalism as a way to enrich existing debates and perspectives, to stimulate thinking, and to generate good feelings. Such an environmentalism is no longer about restrictions. It is about a better life.

Such an effort can build on a wide array of efforts. The field of culture and life has been a vibrant one ever since the Life Reform movement rocked Imperial Germany, and Germany looks different as a result. But the field of culture and life offers new opportunities when we approach it from a political perspective. So far this field had the air of a playground: it was a completely personal choice whether someone wanted to bare it all. However, the field will remain below its potential when we stick to noncommittal advice. There are many ways to frame choices in a way that nudges consumers toward environmental sustainability: taxes for bad products and incentives for good ones, restrictions on sales, product information. Only a few decades ago, food items lacked expiration dates and lists of ingredients, two things that nowadays carry an air of self-evidence. Maybe we can achieve the same for information about a product's carbon footprint?

Lifestyle issues are not beyond politics. Quite the contrary, they are the supreme test for clever regulators. The red-green coalition made some steps in this direction when it introduced ecological taxation, and while these laws were controversial initially, they have survived two changes of government and received widespread acclaim—a good example of how unorthodox measures can turn into routine parts of politics and life. Besides political ambition, it takes reliable information to steer lifestyle choices in the right direction. Information is always important in politics, but it is fast becoming the crucial resource for environmental policy in the twenty-first century. So as we move environmentalism beyond the political sphere, we do not abandon the political field—we may be reinvigorating it.

Beyond the Nation-State

As we have seen, environmentalism was always a concern that crossed borders. But since the 1970s, the international context has grown enormously in significance and complexity. Like most European countries, Germany is now juggling a bewildering array of conventions, treaties, and EU directives, leaving only a few issues where Germans can still make decisions autonomously. Moreover globalization is confronting environmentalism with new challenges, and many NGOs are striving to become global players as well. In short, the internationalization of environmentalism seems like the most obvious development of our time.

However, if the last forty years of German environmentalism show anything, it is that the nation-state remains a significant force. Germany achieved most of its gains in the national context, and support from state administrations was crucial in the rise of Green Germany. There is also no denying that the record of global environmental agreements is not impressive. A quarter-century after its signing, the Montreal Protocol, once thought to be the precedent of global environmental policy, looks more like a fortunate coincidence at the end of the cold war. In global climate negotiations, the standstill is plain for everyone to see.

To be sure, international collaboration remains crucial, as many environmental problems defy national approaches. And yet the globalization of environmentalism is not the natural progression that enthusiastic delegates envisioned at the 1992 Rio summit. The enthusiasm at that meeting is now little more than a fading memory, and after countless summits with meager results, skepticism about environmental diplomacy is increasing. It is not even clear whether global environmental policy is really a boon, rather than an excuse for national inaction; the climate negotiations with their perennial postponements at least raise a certain suspicion in this respect. While international agreements have surely been successful in raising awareness for environmental problems, they have a dismal record when it comes to solutions.

The general approach thus looks uncomfortably reminiscent of the top-down model that Germany pursued in the postwar years: enact ambitious goals and then hope that implementation will somehow work out. It took Germany many years to recognize the "implementation gap" and even more years to deal with it, and that experience cautions against transnational agreements without reliable enforcement mechanisms. Even the European Union, arguably the strongest transnational player that we have, is wrestling with massive implementation problems. The Environment Directorate-General has the power to investigate when it finds implementation deficient, but this approach has lost a lot of its edge through frequent use. At the end of 2010, the Directorate-General had 445 open infringement files under investigation.[9]

The implementation gap is not a mere technicality. After all, implementation decides on whether laws are more than symbolic gestures. Furthermore there is little reason to hope that the implementation gap will somehow disappear over time: the German state maintained its routine of strict principles and lukewarm follow-up for a full century. Implementation is first and foremost a matter of power, and as we have seen, a key lesson from the Green Germany is that successful policies need allies—civic outrage is an important but not a sufficient requirement. Clever politicians, administrators, and businessmen provided key support for environmental causes in Germany. But where are these allies on the international level?

However, international environmental policy is not just about multinational agreements. In recent years we have seen a growing number of nonprofit projects with partners from different countries: for example, carbon offsets to compensate for greenhouse gas emissions from air travel. Finding trustworthy rules and frameworks for these joint endeavors may be among the most urgent needs of international environmentalism, all the more since these projects are bound to increase in number and volume and may soon become a billion dollar business. The potential of these projects is huge, but so are the risks. So far, the worst-case scenario in international environmental policy was deficient implementation. In the future, the worst case will be corruption.

In short, as we move beyond the nation-state, we need to reflect not only on the promises of transnational policy but also on its limitations and side effects. What can we realistically expect from transnational and global measures? And can a country like Germany, both through its prestige and its financial support, become a force for better implementation? Listening to environmentalists, it sometimes seems as if "global" were a synonym of "significant," but that rationale is ultimately self-defeating. It may be time to make a case for local and regional solutions: for quite a number of environmental issues, it would be wise policy to tackle problems on the lowest level possible.

Beyond the West

The globalization of environmental policy has another dimension that deserves a separate discussion. International treaties rest on a common understanding of the problem: it is hard to respond to a challenge when you do not agree on what it is. However, the idea of a joint global agenda has been a dubious one ever since Indira Gandhi's speech in Stockholm 1972. A predominantly rural country on the brink of starvation has a different agenda than industrial and postindustrial societies, and the demands for development and for environmental protection have been sitting uncomfortably next to each other since the 1970s. Like the sword of Damocles, the charge of elitism is hanging over international environmental policy in the Global South.

Rapid industrial development in Asia has made the situation even more complicated. A country like China has an environmental agenda nowadays, but it differs from that of the West. More precisely, it is the condensed version of the agenda that Western countries were dealing with over the course of a hundred years. That makes discussions over priorities even more contentious. How can we ask China to focus on global warming while they are fighting dirt and coal smoke, problems that Western countries themselves prioritized only a few decades ago?

The divergence of agendas is not only a problem for environmental diplomacy, it is also a challenge for the global networking of activists, all the more since the divergence of motives tends to go along with a different social basis. Writing of Southeast Asia, James David Fahn described the gap as follows: "whereas the green movement in the North tends to focus on the middle class, in the South [it is] centered more on the farmers and fishermen who rely on natural resources for their livelihoods . . . ."[10] This rift is particularly significant because environmental protests in the Global South have increased over the last decade. Few environmentalists would doubt that these protests are a welcome development, but at the same time, it also means that we are farther away than ever from a common global agenda.

That makes it all the more advisable to use the word "global" with caution, as it tends to conceal differences in understandings and approaches. We need more transnational debates on views and priorities, but at the moment, the best hope for a truly global agenda may lie in projects that pursue multiple goals. For instance, a forest project may preserve biodiversity, provide employment for the local population, and save greenhouse emissions at the same time. However, designing these multipurpose projects is no trivial matter, all the more since funding schemes tend to favor one aspect only. The debate over climate change in particular has given rise to a narrow focus on greenhouse emissions as if they were all that counts—an intellectual monomania quite at odds with the best traditions of environmental thinking. So, as we develop rules for transnational projects, a key requirement should be to leave as much room as possible for innovative grassroots approaches, and to encourage project partners to aim for multiple goals. It would be painful indeed if the greening of a nation would falter because environmental projects are at odds with international guidelines.

Beyond Pure Green

Among the conditions for success, we saw that in Germany a clear focus was the most important requirement. When environmental issues entered the mainstream in the 1980s, they came with little political baggage. Marxist readings of the ecological crisis were still around, and so was the conservative critique of consumer society, but neither school achieved anything resembling cultural hegemony: those who touted environmental issues could do so simply out of concern for the endangered planet. The environmental sentiments that permeated German society were a pure green, without broader implications and beyond the usual lines of conflict. An early Green Party slogan summarized it nicely: "Neither left nor right, but ahead."[11]

Since the 1990s, the pure green has come under fire from several sides. One of them was the globalization of the environmental debates and the growing importance of non-Western voices. These voices gained weight through groups that criticized the neoliberal model of globalization: organizations such as Attac link ecological concerns with social and economic grievances. Furthermore social inequality reemerged as a political issue in the new millennium, eventually leading to the formation of a new Left Party in Germany in 2007. All of a sudden, the pure green of the 1980s looked terribly naïve.

It was not just about framing the issues. It was also about social status. When German environmentalists focus on environmental issues narrowly, that mirrors a constituency that feels economically secure. The membership of the Green Party provides a case in point. Fully 74 percent of the members are post-materialists as defined by Inglehart, and 25 percent show a mixture of materialist and post-materialist values; only one in a hundred members is a staunch materialist. Among employees who are members of the Green Party, there are only 7 percent blue-collar workers and 48 percent in civil service.[12] In short, environmentalism in the pure green mode was a convenient way to solidify social hierarchies and yet be a concerned, critical citizen.

The environmental movement made some efforts to deal with this blind spot. In 1996 the German League for Environment and Nature Protection (BUND) and the Catholic relief organization MISEREOR presented a joint study on the future of Germany, using the concept of sustainability to link environmental and social concerns. The BUND presented a follow-up study with Protestant partner organizations in 2008.[13] And yet it seems that these efforts are baby steps toward a larger issue: How far can and should environmentalism go? Does it suffice to be more alert to social and economic hardships while maintaining a primary focus on environmental issues? Or is environmentalism bound to become part of a broader movement that pushes for social, economic, and ecological justice? It is quite possible that a few years from now, justice will be the word that unites diverse concerns in the same way that ecology did in the 1970s and 1980s.

Justice is a discourse issue if ever there was one. However, there are also many opportunities to link environmentalism and justice in practice. One stands out in particular: depressed urban areas. The gulf between rich and poor urban quarters has grown enormously over the last decades, and Germans are slowly realizing that they have veritable ghettos where unemployment, poverty, and ethnic discrimination run rampant. It will take many things to stop this trend, but why can't environmental regeneration be one of them? Environmental justice is a global issue, but it starts back home.

Beyond Corporatism

Throughout the twentieth century, corporatism was a defining feature of German environmental policy. Rather than taking decisions, officials delegated complicated issues to committees of experts and lobbyists, which eventually came up with a solution that all parties could live with. As students of political science know, corporatism has a tendency to foster corruption, allowing backroom deals that go at the expense of those not present. Against that background, one can argue that corporatist approaches have generally worked quite well for German environmentalism, especially when the state kept a close watch on negotiations and threatened to intervene if things went out of hand. For one thing, Germany was spared the bitter conflicts over technical standards that have characterized environmental regulation in the United States. Whereas American rules and regulations frequently become subject to court challenges that delay implementation for years, Germans rarely spat over these issues in public.[14] It is common practice to negotiate over new standards with industry in an effort to win their approval. Not everyone may like the result, but the vested interests at least had a fair chance to voice their concerns.

It is interesting that we rarely find general statements on the merits of corporatist regulation throughout the twentieth century. Corporatism was an administrative practice rather than an official policy, with officials opting for negotiations in an ad hoc fashion. Environmental problems are notoriously complex, they require expert knowledge, and they often call for a compromise between different parties—so why not leave it to these parties to develop the compromise autonomously? For officials wrestling with difficult problems, corporatism was the path of least resistance.

In the 1970s, it looked as if corporatism was doomed. Faced with increasing protest, industry realized that environmentalism would demand major investments, making negotiations much more contentious. In the conflict over nuclear power, opinions clashed in a way that made a compromise virtually impossible. It appeared probable that Germany would follow the path of the United States, where environmentalism had instilled a shift toward an antagonistic mode of regulation around 1970, effectively debunking a tradition of cooperative, expert-driven regulation that looped back to the Progressive Era. Germany did see a number of hefty conflicts as well, including conflicts with corporate heavyweights such as the lignite and chemical industries, and yet corporatist negotiations remained a prominent feature of environmental policy. Over time, the insiders proved willing to invite NGOs to the negotiating table, and appointing environmentalists to boards and committees is nowadays part of political business as usual.

Corporatism reached its apogee when the red-green coalition invited its friends from the environmental community to all sorts of meetings. However, the experience provokes mixed feelings in retrospect. During the red-green years, the environmental movement looked strangely tame, as meetings consumed much of its resources. Furthermore corporatist deals have a tendency to placate public controversies. It is obviously against the rules to negotiate a compromise behind closed doors and then attack the result in public. Of course, environmentalists could always leave the backrooms and launch protests, but they were hesitant to do so. Environmental campaigns lost much of their vigor, and particularly their critical edge toward official policy. When protest gathered in the run-up to the Copenhagen climate summit in 2009, the campaigners' goals looked virtually identical to that of the German government.

The ambiguous experience with corporatism is probably no German peculiarity. All over the world, it has become common practice to invite NGOs to meetings, and scores of environmentalists have been appointed to political office; Yolanda Kakabadse and Wangari Maathai, who started their careers in civil society and eventually became environmental minister and assistant minister in Ecuador and Kenya, are two of the best-known examples. It is always a balancing act, a trade-off that provides environmentalism with influence at the expense of independence. How much can environmentalism rely on insider deals without losing its soul? In the German case, parts of the environmental movement are dangerously close to a corporatist entanglement where they can no longer say the word "no."

Beyond Solutions

In retrospect, German environmental history looks like a progression from simple problems toward ever more intricate ones. To be sure, simple problems can keep civic groups busy for years, as the struggle over the Wutach Gorge during the 1950s serves to attest. But for all the bitterness of that conflict, there was at least a clear solution in sight—the preservation of the gorge. The situation was similar when it came to the pollution of air and water. Filters and sewage treatment plants were proven technologies. The challenge was to make sure that industrialists and municipalities were using them.

Over time, environmental concerns moved on to more costly issues. Once every coal-fired power plant had proper fly ash collection, sulfur dioxide emissions came into view, a problem that was more difficult and expensive to solve. As we have seen, it took a prolonged struggle and the fear of widespread deforestation to strong-arm utilities into the construction of scrubbers. The situation was similar with catalytic converters in cars and industrial safety in chemical factories, and yet the objections were mostly of a financial nature. In terms of technology, the solution was easy. As soon as the technological fix became mandatory, the environmentalists could declare victory.

The existence of technological solutions was an important precondition for the ecological 1980s. By the late 1970s, German environmental policy was wrestling with a backlog of technological options that were feasible but expensive. That brought environmentalists into a rather favorable position: they did not have to bother about finding solutions and could devote all energies to fostering public outrage. Should we really refrain from using these advanced technologies simply because they cost the polluters money? For a civic movement, it was the perfect case to argue, and once the backlog began to wither and industrialists were hurriedly retrofitting their equipment, German environmentalists could celebrate a string of spectacular victories. For a few years, environmentalism looked amazingly successful.

However, German environmentalists eventually ran out of problems with a quick technological fix. Problems like climate change and biodiversity defy simple solutions, and the same is true for lesser known problems like fine particulates and soil conservation. One can legitimately doubt that humankind can actually solve these problems in the way that we could solve the problem of sulfur emissions. As it stands, it seems that the best we can do is to keep these problems within certain limits. While the environmental policy of the past was about solutions, the environmental policy of the future is about management.

We have seen that transition in policy debates of the last two decades, particular in discussions over global warming. However, if we see that against the background of the ecological 1980s, it is clear that new policies are only part of the answer. After all, the political field is just one of the three fields of environmentalism, and chances are that policies will remain below their potential if they do not merge with trends in civil society and culture. Specifically, how can we combine a management approach to environmental problems with the craving of civic leagues for the experience of success? And how should environmentalists react when a purported solution such as the Kyoto Protocol turns into a liability for future policies?

On March 9, 2010, the front page of *The New York Times* featured two articles on environmental issues. One dealt with the crisis of the solar industry in Spain. The previous September, the Spanish government had abruptly changed its solar policy because generous subsidies had encouraged the installation of low-quality, poorly designed panels, providing an object lesson on the intricacies of promoting renewable energies. The other article dealt with the illegal trade in whale meat. The team behind the documentary film *The Cove*, which had won an Academy Award the previous Sunday, had conducted a covert operation in a top-end sushi restaurant in Santa Monica. As *The Cove* had chronicled environmental activists in their struggle against dolphin hunting in Japan, the team used secret cameras and microphones to uncover a terrible truth: the place was serving whale meat.[15]

The interesting thing about this front page is that it mirrors two possible futures of environmentalism. Whales are always sure to generate public excitement, and the covert operation was a guaranteed success: the restaurant was closed within a fortnight. In contrast, the details of renewable energy policies are inherently boring, and yet they are certainly far more significant for environmental sustainability than a few rich people eating whale meat. In short, the combination illustrated a key dilemma of environmentalism today: the important issues are not charismatic, and the charismatic issues are not important.

It may be rewarding to keep this in mind as Germany is getting underway with its post-Fukushima energy transition. Policies for the promotion of renewable energy may backfire, and in a way already have; just a few years after the Spanish bust, the German solar industry is currently facing a similar crisis. And yet sophisticated policies are only one part of the answer. Another is to get environmental NGOs excited about these things, and the broad public to care. Environmentalism remains a delicate web of politics, civil society, and culture, and the interactions of these turfs defy simple solutions. A management approach to environmental problems is a perennial balancing act that requires careful attention to interactions and unintended side effects, and a readiness to respond and modify approaches. As Germany is moving ahead on renewable energy, it may provide some insights into what to do and what to avoid.

Stay tuned.

How Green After All? An Epilogue

As it happens, this book is also a farewell to my country of birth. The University of Birmingham offered me a position while this book was under review, and my move to the British Isles was just weeks away when I sent the final version to press. For all the excitement that a new job and a new country offer, these situations also bring to mind things one will miss. The distance between Munich and Birmingham is only about a thousand kilometers, and even less from the place where I grew up, but national boundaries can make a difference. For one thing, I will move from a country that is shutting down its nuclear reactors to a country that is currently banking on a nuclear revival.

However, personal sentiments are a less than perfect guide when it comes to a judgment on a country's overall performance on environmental issues. The issue of how green Germany really is has followed us through this book, and it deserves a summary assessment by way of conclusion. And yet such a general statement must inevitably wrestle with a bewildering range of problems and parameters. A country's environmental profile comprises a vast array of divergent aspects: pollution, waste disposal, biodiversity, carbon footprint, and so on. Furthermore, such an endeavor runs a significant risk of imposing a specific environmental agenda. For instance, there are still a few environmentalists around who think that nuclear power might be green.

Fortunately, other experts have already pondered these quandaries at length, and scholars can nowadays choose from several sustainability rankings for the nations of the world. The gold standard is the Environmental Performance Index, not least due to the prestige of its sponsors: it is a joint venture of the Yale Center for Environmental Law and Policy and Columbia University's Center for International Earth Science Information Network in collaboration with the World Economic Forum and the Joint Research Centre of the European Commission. The project has evolved over more than a decade, and the latest edition of 2012 looks at 22 performance indicators for 132 countries.[1] Ranked as number 11 in the world, Germany did well in this round, though it trailed other European countries such as France, Italy, and Sweden. The countries at the top of the list were Switzerland, Latvia, and Norway.[2]

Germany earned its high marks through its strong performance in environmental health. It received top scores for the quality of air and water, which meets nicely with the findings of this book: as we have seen, the fight against pollution was one of the defining features of German environmentalism since the 1970s. Germany also received top scores in the biodiversity and habitat category, the result of more than a century of state-centered nature conservation. The makers of the Environmental Performance Index were less impressed with its agriculture and its forests, two issues where environmental demands have met strong resistance. The result obviously mirrors the profile of German environmentalism: the country did well overall because of decades of environmental activism.[3]

Germany performed even better in a report that the Environmental Rating Agency released in time for the Rio+20 Earth Summit in June 2012. Researched and published by Matt Prescott, the report uses the terminology of credit ratings to evaluate environmental sustainability for G20 member countries. Germany received an A+, which is four scales below the coveted AAA rating that designates top performance. Nonetheless, that made it the best among 19 large countries all over the world. To be sure, with only 12 indicators and its focus on G20 member states, the report is less impressive than the Environmental Performance Index, but coming out on top among the major economies of the world is surely no small achievement. However, the report stresses that even top ranking nations were "patchy in their environmental performance," with Germany performing worst in relation to its forests—an interesting finding for the much-touted motherland of sustainable forestry. Another significant result is that Germany's power stations are "surprisingly inefficient" compared with those of other countries.[4]

Germanwatch and Climate Action Network Europe publish an annual ranking that focuses on a single issue: climate change. In a group of 58 countries, the 2013 index puts Germany on rank eight, which is even better than it sounds. The Climate Change Performance Index leaves ranks one to three unfilled as a reminder that no country is doing enough against climate change. Germany is thus effectively number five after Denmark, Sweden, Portugal, and Switzerland. The report puts high hopes on Germany's energy transition, arguing that it "could prove to be a role model for other countries to reduce their fossil fuel consumption." At the same time, it notes that Germany performs below average in the carbon and energy efficiency category, underscoring the Environmental Rating Agency's observation about power plants. For a country that excels in engineering, it is somewhat embarrassing that it leaves "its huge potential for efficiency improvements untapped."[5]

Of course, these indexes are open to discussion, and one can quibble endlessly about the choice of parameters and their relative weight. However, the greater worry is that indexes focus on figures: many aspects of the Green Germany defy quantification. For instance, it is surely a testament to the strength of environmental sentiments that Germany reacted more strongly to the Fukushima nuclear disaster than any other country in the world, including Japan. Or take the Green Party and influential NGOs such as Germanwatch that reach out far beyond Central Europe: the strength of Germany's green civil society is not admired elsewhere for nothing. And then there is the field of culture and life: whole grain bread, muesli, sandals, and a growing popularity of a vegetarian diet show the enduring allure of green issues. You can safely take a dip in the Rhine at Düsseldorf even though you are swimming downstream from the largest concentration of chemical factories in Europe (though, ever-vigilant, authorities warn you to watch out for ship traffic). And you do not even need a bathing suit.

To be sure, green lifestyles are not omnipresent in contemporary German society. It only takes a look at a major shopping street on a Saturday afternoon to realize that Germany has not foresworn consumerism. And yet environmentalism has left a permanent mark on what Germans eat and buy: for example, the market share of organic food has grown continuously for many years. Bike lanes and decent public transportation make cars an option rather than a must, and clean and safe parks provide urban residents with a green refuge. It is crucial to recognize these strands of green even while they are hard to put into numbers. In fact, when it comes to the things that make Germany a good place to live (and, on a personal note, the things that I will miss), it was frequently environmentalism that made the difference.

Furthermore the Green Germany looks stable for the foreseeable future. The typical threats to environmentalism are either small or completely absent. No significant political force is seeking to dismantle Germany's environmental achievements, and it is hard to imagine a culture war over green issues. The

Green Party and environmental NGOs have a large and diverse base of members and donors. Radical environmentalists are few in numbers and receive scant attention in the general public. Green technology is a firmly established branch of business that no sane politician would want to jeopardize. The ordo-liberal framework of the German economy and its penchant for long-range investments make rapid swings of the governing philosophy even more unlikely.

So is Germany, if not *the* greenest nation, at least a country that environmentalists should look at closely? Enthusiasts should probably take note of the many caveats throughout this book before heading to language school. After all, the amazing thing about the Green Germany is that it stands in a strangely disconnected relationship to gross environmental liabilities: lignite mining, reckless automobilism, unrestrained suburban growth, long-distance flights to sunny beaches, and a meat-heavy mainstream diet. Germans find it surprisingly hard to connect the dots—probably a common syndrome in Western societies, and yet a remarkable one for a country that made environmentalism part of its patriotic creed. In any case, the gap between meaning well and doing well is wide on many issues and breathtaking on some, and the notion of the greenest nation probably says more about those who embrace it than about German realities. Indeed any other result would have been surprising. The hope for a country that excels in everything environmental is probably nothing more than a green midsummer night's dream.

The caveats are bigger still when it comes to whether Germany will continue to improve. This book has argued that German environmentalism is in crisis (though, admittedly, on a pretty high level), and it is interesting to note that the previously cited studies share this concern. Matt Prescott's Environmental Rating Agency declared that "there are relatively few 'quick wins' left" for Germany: future gains would hinge on changes in personal consumption and more renewable and efficient technology.[6] The Environmental Performance Index even put it into figures when it ranked Germany as number 56 in its trend index, meaning that in 2012 there were 55 countries in the world that were improving faster than Germany. Of course, innovation becomes harder when you are doing well, but the comments underscore one of the key arguments of this study: the times of great leaps lie in the past. A repetition of the ecological 1980s with their spectacular series of dramatic successes is even more unlikely than a collapse of the Green Germany.

Still, the German achievements are remarkable, particularly if we look beyond the European continent. The United States performed notably lower than Germany in all three rankings: it was the 49th country on the Environmental Performance Index, fourth on the Environmental Rating Agency's G20 list, and 43rd on the Climate Change Performance Index. Canada performed no better, ranking 37th, fifth, and 58th, respectively—with the latter score being particularly embarrassing since Canada could only beat Kazakhstan, Saudi Arabia, and Iran on climate change. And then there are countries like the Russian Federation and China that consistently rank close to the bottom. However, the country whose performance intrigued me the most was my new home, the United Kingdom: it consistently paired with Germany as if the makers of these indexes wanted to protect this author from an upcoming bout of homesickness. Great Britain was two ranks ahead of Germany in the Environmental Performance Index, second after Germany among the G20, and two ranks behind in the Climate Change Performance Index.

The similarity in performance is arguably of more than individual interest. Germany and Great Britain make for an interesting set of contrasts, and yet they arrive at comparable results. For example, the sitting governments diverge not only over nuclear technology but also over the promotion of renewable energy. Other contrasts show up in everyday life: an average German's look at a typical British window, with its thin glass and amateurish insulation, commonly brings up a deep longing for German craftsmanship. And that is just the latest twist in a curiously entangled history. When Germany indulged in the ecological 1980s, Britain's environmental policy gained the country an international reputation as "the dirty man of Europe."[7] Yet another generation earlier, the situation was different again: around 1960, with London smog on the decline, large swaths of the land under protection, aggressive land use planning, and a number of grand, long-standing conservation leagues, Great Britain was probably the greenest nation in Europe. Surely no one would have thought that about Germany back then.

In the end, that underscores one of the basic contentions of this study. There is no uniform model or a standard path that nations can follow—the world is simply too complicated for that. What we do have is countries that realize their environmental potential with varying degrees of success. After decades of neglect, Germany finally got its act together in the 1970s and 1980s and realized much of its environmental potential; Great Britain followed another path toward a similar environmental performance. (And, lest we forget, the gap between top and average performers is surely smaller than that between the best Western nations and long-range environmental sustainability.) The path toward sustainability is not just about good ideas—environmentalism has long had an abundance of those—but also about power, political resources, and clever coalitions. Germany showed a quarter-century ago how things can come together in ways both planned and unplanned, and it is still profiting from the experience. There is no reason why other countries cannot achieve the same feat.

Notes

Foreword

1. Donald Worster, *The Wealth of Nature: Environmental History and the Ecological Imagination* (New York: Oxford University Press, 1993), 142–43.

2. Frank Uekötter, *The Greenest Nation? A New History of German Environmentalism* (Cambridge: MIT Press, 2014), 104.

3. Ronald Inglehart, *The Silent Revolution: Changing Values and Political Styles among Western Publics* (Princeton: Princeton University Press, 1977).

Chapter 1

1. http://www.oecd.org/document/53/0,3746,en_2649_37465_50475829_1_1_1_37465,00.html and http://www.oecd.org/document/6/0,3746,en_2649_37465_50066118_1_1_1_37465,00.html (accessed May 21, 2013).

2. Renewable Energy Policy Network for the 21st Century (REN21), *Renewables 2012. Global Status Report*, p. 7, available online at http://www.map.ren21.net/GSR/GSR2012_low.pdf (accessed May 21, 2013).

3. http://www.whitehouse.gov/the-press-office/2012/01/24/remarks-president-state-union-address (accessed May 21, 2013).

4. For a discussion of Bramwell's thesis, see Frank Uekötter, *The Green and the Brown: A History of Conservation in Nazi Germany* (Cambridge, UK: Cambridge University Press, 2006), 202n.

5. The following remarks are a condensed version of my "Consigning Environmentalism to History? Remarks on the Place of the Environmental Movement in Modern History," *RCC Perspectives* 7 (2011).

6. Roderick Nash, *Wilderness and the American Mind* (New Haven: Yale University Press, 1967).

7. Brian William Clapp, *An Environmental History of Britain since the Industrial Revolution* (London: Longman, 1994); David Evans, *A History of Nature Conservation in Britain* (London: Routledge, 1997); John Sheail, *An Environmental History of Twentieth-Century Britain* (Basingstoke, UK: Palgrave, 2002); Alon Tal, *Pollution in a Promised Land: An Environmental History of Israel* (Berkeley: University of California Press, 2002).

8. Rolf Peter Sieferle, *Fortschrittsfeinde? Opposition gegen Technik und Industrie von der Romantik bis zur Gegenwart* (Munich: Beck, 1984); Ulrich Linse, *Ökopax und Anarchie: Eine Geschichte der ökologischen Bewegungen in Deutschland* (Munich: dtv, 1986); Jost Hermand, *Grüne Utopien in Deutschland: Zur Geschichte des ökologischen Bewußtseins* (Frankfurt: Fischer, 1991); Raymond H. Dominick, *The Environmental Movement in Germany: Prophets and Pioneers, 1871–1971* (Bloomington: Indiana University Press, 1992); Franz-Josef Brüggemeier, *Tschernobyl, April 26, 1986: Die ökologische Herausforderung* (Munich: dtv, 1998); Joachim Radkau, *Die Ära der Ökologie: Eine Weltgeschichte* (Munich: Beck, 2011).

9. Dominick, *Environmental Movement*.

10. Several scholars have criticized the draft for not offering a clear definition of environmentalism. They had a point: I discuss approaches toward a deeper understanding of environmentalism, but I remain vague as to what it is. But maybe that is an advantage? My impression is that a clear-cut definition of environmentalism (a word without a German equivalent, by the way) would foster the feeling of cognitive certainty that I intend to challenge. Environmentalism is changing, and we should not pretend otherwise.

11. Sylvia Hood Washington, Paul C. Rosier, Heather Goodall, eds., *Echoes from the Poisoned Well: Global Memories of Environmental Injustice* (Lanham, MD: Lexington Books, 2006); Joan Martinez-Alier, *The Environmentalism of the Poor: A Study of Ecological Conflicts and Valuation* (Northhampton, MA: Elgar, 2002); Chad Montrie, *A People's History of Environmentalism in the United States* (London: Continuum, 2011). See also Martin V. Melosi, "Environ-

mental Justice, Political Agenda Setting, and the Myths of History," Melosi, ed., *Effluent America: Cities, Industry, Energy and the Environment* (Pittsburgh: University of Pittsburgh Press, 2001), 238–62.

12. Robert Gottlieb, *Forcing the Spring: The Transformation of the American Environmental Movement* (Washington, DC: Island Press, 1993).

13. Anthony Giddens, *The Politics of Climate Change* (Cambridge, UK: Polity, 2009), 50.

14. For a bold demonstration of how environmental history can stimulate general history, see Mark Fiege, *The Republic of Nature: An Environmental History of the United States* (Seattle: University of Washington Press, 2012).

15. For introductions to Bourdieu's social theory, see David Swartz, *Culture and Power: The Sociology of Pierre Bourdieu* (Chicago: University of Chicago Press, 1997); Derek Robbins, *The Work of Pierre Bourdieu: Recognizing Society* (Boulder: Westview Press, 1991); Richard Jenkins, *Pierre Bourdieu* (London: Routledge, 1992).

16. I make no pretense of discussing the three fields equally in this book. I have focused mostly on the political and civic field because I think that they are of greatest interest to international readers. My goal is to highlight that culture and life need a place in the history of environmentalism, rather than to provide a satisfactory discussion of this field. For a pioneering collection of essays, see Axel Goodbody, ed., *The Culture of German Environmentalism: Anxieties, Visions, Realities* (New York: Berghahn Books, 2002). See also Axel Goodbody, *Nature, Technology and Cultural Change in Twentieth-Century German Literature: The Challenge of Ecocriticism* (Basingstoke, UK: Palgrave Macmillan, 2007).

17. Pierre Bourdieu, *Distinction: A Social Critique of the Judgment of Taste* (Cambridge: Harvard University Press, 1984).

18. Badisches Generallandesarchiv Karlsruhe Abt. 233, no. 3029, Kaiserlich Deutsche Botschaft in Frankreich to Reichskanzler von Bethmann Hollweg, November 11, 1909.

19. Richard J. Evans, *Death in Hamburg: Society and Politics in the Cholera Years 1830–1910* (Oxford: Clarendon Press, 1987), 118, 133.

20. Daniel T. Rodgers, *Atlantic Crossings: Social Politics in a Progressive Age* (Cambridge: Belknap Press of Harvard University Press, 1998), 131n.

21. Bernhard Gissibl, Sabine Höhler, Patrick Kupper, eds., *Civilizing Nature: National Parks in Global Historical Perspective* (New York: Berghahn Books, 2012).

22. See Horst Gründer, ed., . . . *da und dort ein junges Deutschland gründen: Rassismus, Kolonien und kolonialer Gedanke vom 16. bis zum 20. Jahrhundert* (Munich: dtv, 1999), 147–49.

23. Thaddeus Raymond Sunseri, *Wilding the Ax: State Forestry and Social Conflict in Tanzania, 1820–2000* (Athens: Ohio University Press, 2009); Thomas M. Lekan, "'Serengeti Shall Not Die': Bernhard Grzimek, Wildlife Film, and the Making of a Tourist Landscape in East Africa," *German History* 29 (2011): 224–64; Bernhard Gissibl, "A Bavarian Serengeti: Space, Race and Time in the Entangled History of Nature Conservation in East Africa and Germany," Gissibl et al., *Civilizing Nature*, 102–19; Franziska Torma, *Eine Naturschutzkampagne in der Ära Adenauer: Bernhard Grzimeks Afrikafilme in den Medien der 50er Jahre* (Munich: Meidenbauer, 2004).

24. Julia Obertreis, "Der 'Angriff auf die Wüste' in Zentralasien: Zur Umweltgeschichte der Sowjetunion," *Osteuropa* 58, 4–5 (2008): 37–56.

25. David Blackbourn, *The Conquest of Nature: Water, Landscape, and the Making of Germany* (New York: Norton, 2006).

26. Michael Bess, *The Light-Green Society: Ecology and Technological Modernity in France, 1960–2000* (Chicago: University of Chicago Press, 2003), 4.

27. Frank Uekötter, *The Age of Smoke: Environmental Policy in Germany and the United States, 1880–1970* (Pittsburgh: University of Pittsburgh Press, 2009).

Chapter 2

1. I discuss this periodization more extensively in my *Umweltgeschichte im 19. und 20. Jahrhundert* (Munich: Oldenbourg, 2007), 14–23.

2. Andreas Knaut, *Zurück zur Natur! Die Wurzeln der Ökologiebewegung* (Jahrbuch für Naturschutz und Landschaftspflege, suppl. 1, Greven: Kilda-Verlag, 1993); Friedemann Schmoll, *Erinnerung an die Natur: Die Geschichte des Naturschutzes im deutschen Kaiserreich* (Frankfurt: Campus, 2004).

3. Westfälisches Archivamt Münster Best. 717 Zug. 23/1999 Natur-schutzverein, Satzung des Westfälischen Naturschutzvereins of 1934, p. 4.

4. Vgl. Tal, *Pollution*.

5. Schmoll, *Erinnerung*, 301–37.

6. Quoted after Walther Schönichen, *Naturschutz, Heimatschutz: Ihre Begründung durch Ernst Rudorff, Hugo Conwentz und ihre Vorläufer* (Stuttgart: Wissenschaftliche Verlagsgesellschaft, 1954), 279.

7. Miriam Zerbel, *Tierschutz im Kaiserreich: Ein Beitrag zur Geschichte des Vereinswesens* (Frankfurt: Lang, 1993), 83, 88.

8. Zerbel, "Tierschutz und Antivivisektion," Diethart Kerbs, Jürgen Reulecke, eds., *Handbuch der deutschen Reformbewegungen, 1880–1933* (Wuppertal: Hammer, 1998), 41; Mieke Roscher, *Ein Königreich für Tiere: Die Geschichte der britischen Tierrechtsbewegung* (Marburg: Tectum-Verlag, 2009).

9. Schmoll, *Erinnerung*, 198–201.

10. Charles S. Maier, "Consigning the Twentieth Century to History: Alternative Narratives for the Modern Era," *American Historical Review* 105 (2000): 807–831.

11. Alfred Runte, *Yosemite: The Embattled Wilderness* (Lincoln: University of Nebraska Press, 1990), 99.

12. Karl Ditt, "Vom Natur- zum Umweltschutz? England 1949 bis 1990," Franz-Josef Brüggemeier, Jens Ivo Engels, eds., *Natur- und Umweltschutz nach 1945: Konzepte, Konflikte, Kompetenzen* (Frankfurt: Campus, 2005), 38–61; 39n.

13. Bundesarchiv B 245/214, p. 50.

14. G. A. Brouwer, *The Organisation of Nature Protection in the Various Countries* (Special Publication of the American Committee for International Wild Life Protection no. 9, Cambridge: n.p., 1938), 31.

15. Ulrich Linse, "'Der Raub des Rheingoldes': Das Wasserkraftwerk Laufenburg," Linse et al., eds., *Von der Bittschrift zur Platzbesetzung: Konflikte um technische Großprojekte. Laufenburg, Walchensee, Wyhl, Wackersdorf* (Berlin: Dietz, 1988), 11–62.

16. For an overview on conservation outside Prussia, see Schmoll, *Erinnerung*, 161–71.

17. Walther Schönichen, "'Wir wollen einen Naturschutzpark gründen und . . .,'" *Naturschutz* 15 (1934): 137–39; 137.

18. Leo von Boxberger, "Naturschutzbürokratie," *Naturschutz* 7 (1926): 187–90; 187; Boxberger, "Wege zum Naturschutz," *Naturschutz* 3 (1922): 5–8; 6.

19. Bess, *Light-Green Society*, 68.

20. Linda Flint McClelland, *Building the National Parks: Historic Landscape Design and Construction* (Baltimore: Johns Hopkins University Press, 1998), 110–12.

21. Susanne Falk, *Der Sauerländische Gebirgsverein: "Vielleicht sind wir die Modernen von übermorgen"* (Bonn: Bouvier, 1990), 113.

22. Hans-Werner Frohn, "Naturschutz macht Staat—Staat macht Naturschutz. Von der Staatlichen Stelle für Naturdenkmalpflege in Preußen bis zum Bundesamt für Naturschutz 1906 bis 2006—Eine Institutionengeschichte," Frohn, Friedemann Schmoll, eds., *Natur und Staat: Staatlicher Naturschutz in Deutschland, 1906–2006* (Bonn-Bad Godesberg: Bundesamt für Naturschutz, 2006), 85–313; 112.

23. Generallandesarchiv Karlsruhe Abt. 235 no. 48254, Eingabe an die deutschen Regierungen, undated (around 1913).

24. Ibid.

25. Stenographische Berichte über die Verhandlungen des Reichstags, XI. Legislaturperiode, 1st session, vol. 1 (Berlin, 1904), 774. As one might guess, black was the signature color of political Catholicism in Germany.

26. Stenographische Berichte über die Verhandlungen des Preußischen Hauses der Abgeordneten, 21st Legislaturperiode, 4th session 1911, vol. 2 (Berlin, 1911), 2679.

27. Peter Thorsheim, *Inventing Pollution: Coal, Smoke, and Culture in Britain since 1800* (Athens: Ohio University Press, 2006), 89, 103n.

28. David Stradling, *Smokestacks and Progressives: Environmentalists, Engineers and Air Quality in America, 1881–1951* (Baltimore: Johns Hopkins University Press, 1999); Uekötter, *Age of Smoke*.

29. Stadtarchiv Frankfurt am Main R 1528, vol. 1, Martin Göpfert to Magistrat der Stadt Frankfurt, November 19, 1928.

30. *Sitzungsberichte des Vereins zur Beförderung des Gewerbfleißes, 1899* (Berlin, 1899), 134.

31. Uekötter, *Age of Smoke.*

32. Bundesarchiv R 154/92, Fachausschuss für Staubtechnik, Bericht über die Vollsitzung on March 19, 1930.

33. Jürgen Büschenfeld, *Flüsse und Kloaken: Umweltfragen im Zeitalter der Industrialisierung (1870–1918)* (Stuttgart: Klett-Cotta, 1997); Evans, *Death in Hamburg*; Wolfgang R. Krabbe, *Die deutsche Stadt im 19. und 20. Jahrhundert: Eine Einführung* (Göttingen: Vandenhoeck & Ruprecht, 1989).

34. Rodgers, *Atlantic Crossings*, 123.

35. On Stöckhard and his research tradition, see Arne Andersen, *Historische Technikfolgenabschätzung am Beispiel des Metallhüttenwesens und der Chemieindustrie, 1850–1933* (Stuttgart: Steiner, 1996). See also Martin Bemmann, *Beschädigte Vegetation und sterbender Wald: Zur Entstehung eines Umweltproblems in Deutschland, 1893–1970* (Göttingen: Vandenhoeck & Ruprecht, 2012), though his discussion of science is somewhat constrained by the book's focus.

36. *Beiträge zur Naturdenkmalpflege* 1 (1910): 171.

37. John Alexander Williams, *Turning to Nature in Germany: Hiking, Nudism, and Conservation, 1900–1940* (Stanford: Stanford University Press, 2007); Judith Baumgartner, *Ernährungsreform—Antwort auf Industrialisierung und Ernährungswandel: Ernährungsreform als Teil der Lebensreformbewegung am Beispiel der Siedlung und des Unternehmens Eden seit 1893* (Frankfurt: Lang, 1992), 125–204.

38. Diethart Kerbs, Jürgen Reulecke, eds., *Handbuch der deutschen Reformbewegungen, 1880–1933* (Wuppertal: Hammer, 1998) and Kai Buchholz et al., eds., *Die Lebensreform: Entwürfe zur Neugestaltung von Leben und Kunst um 1900*, 2 vol. (Darmstadt: Häusser, 2001).

39. Eric J. Hobsbawm, *The Age of Extremes: The Short Twentieth Century, 1914–1991* (London: Michael Joseph, 1994).

40. Rubner, "Das durch Artilleriegeschosse verursachte Fichtensterben," *Mitteilungen der Bayerischen Botanischen Gesellschaft zur Erforschung der heimischen Flora* 3:13 (January 1, 1916): 273–76.

41. Bayerisches Hauptstaatsarchiv München MWi 654, Bundesrat, Tagung 1918, Drucksache no. 121.

42. Stadtarchiv Erfurt 1–2/506–382, p. 42.

43. Institut für Umweltgeschichte und Regionalentwicklung, ed., *Lexikon der Naturschutzbeauftragten*. Vol. 3: *Naturschutzgeschichte*

und Naturschutzbeauftragte in Berlin und Brandenburg (Friedland: Steffen, 2010), 28.

44. Sitzungsberichte der verfassunggebenden Preußischen Landes-versammlung, Tagung 1919/21, vol. 9 (Berlin, 1921), 11782.

45. Dirk Lukaßen, *Grüne Koalitionen: Naturkonzepte und Natur-schutzpraxis in der Weimarer Republik* (Siegburg: Rheinlandia, 2010), 51.

46. Richard Hölzl, "Naturschutz in Bayern zwischen Staat und Zivil-gesellschaft: Vom liberalen Aufbruch bis zur Eingliederung in das NS-Regime, 1913 bis 1945," *Bund Naturschutz Forschung* 11 (2013): 21–60.

47. Badisches Generallandesarchiv Karlsruhe Abt. 235, no. 48254, Der Reichsminister des Innern to the Landesregierungen, July 2, 1932.

48. Thomas M. Lekan, *Imagining the Nation in Nature: Landscape Preservation and German Identity, 1885–1945* (Cambridge: Harvard University Press, 2003), 111.

49. Franz-Josef Brüggemeier, Thomas Rommelspacher, *Blauer Him-mel über der Ruhr: Geschichte der Umwelt im Ruhrgebiet, 1840–1990* (Essen: Klartext, 1992), 51.

50. Bundesarchiv R 154/92, Zwanglose Mitteilungen des Fachaus-schusses für Staubtechnik im Verein deutscher Ingenieure no. 1 (June, 1928), p. 1.

51. Ibid., Fachausschuß für Staubtechnik, Bericht über die Vollsit-zung on November 5, 1931.

52. Stadtarchiv Herne VII/247 a and b, pp. 68–69.

53. Rudolf Steiner, *Spiritual Foundations for the Renewal of Agri-culture: A Course of Lectures held at Koberwitz, Silesia, June 7 to 16, 1924* (Kimberton, Pennsylvania: Bio-Dynamic Farming and Garden-ing Association, 1993).

54. Frank Uekötter, *Die Wahrheit ist auf dem Feld: Eine Wissensge-schichte der deutschen Landwirtschaft* (Göttingen: Vandenhoeck & Ruprecht, 2010), 232–46. Quotation 233.

55. Gunter Vogt, *Entstehung und Entwicklung des ökologischen Landbaus* (Bad Dürkheim: SÖL, 2000); Uwe Werner, *Anthroposo-phen in der Zeit des Nationalsozialismus (1933–1945)* (Munich: Oldenbourg, 1999); Helmut Zander, *Anthroposophie in Deutsch-land: Theosophische Weltanschauung und gesellschaftliche Praxis,*

1884–1945, 2 vol. (Göttingen: Vandenhoeck & Ruprecht, 2007); Peter Staudenmaier, "Organic Farming in Nazi Germany: The Politics of Biodynamic Agriculture, 1933–1945," *Environmental History* 18 (2013): 383–11.

56. For some of the studies that support the following remarks, see Franz-Josef Brüggemeier, Mark Cioc, Thomas Zeller, eds., *How Green Were the Nazis? Nature, Environment, and Nation in the Third Reich* (Athens: Ohio University Press, 2005); Joachim Radkau, Frank Uekötter, eds., *Naturschutz und Nationalsozialismus* (Frankfurt: Campus, 2003); Willi Oberkrome, *"Deutsche Heimat": Nationale Konzeption und regionale Praxis von Naturschutz, Landschaftsgestaltung und Kulturpolitik in Westfalen-Lippe und Thüringen, 1900–1960* (Paderborn: Schöningh, 2004); Thomas Zeller, *Driving Germany: The Landscape of the German Autobahn, 1930–1970* (New York: Berghahn Books, 2007); Uekötter, *The Green and the Brown*; Lekan, *Imagining the Nation in Nature*.

57. Anna Bramwell, *Blood and Soil: Walther Darré and Hitler's Green Party* (Abbotsbrook: Kensal Press, 1985), and Anna Bramwell, *Ecology in the 20th Century: A History* (New Haven: Yale University Press, 1989), 198.

58. Walther Schönichen, "Appell der deutschen Landschaft an den Arbeitsdienst," *Naturschutz* 14 (1933): 145–49.

59. Susanne Falk, "'Eine Notwendigkeit, uns innerlich umzustellen, liege nicht vor': Kontinuität und Diskontinuität in der Auseinandersetzung des Sauerländischen Gebirgsvereins mit Heimat und Moderne, 1918–1960," Matthias Frese, Michael Prinz, eds., *Politische Zäsuren und Gesellschaftlicher Wandel im 20. Jahrhundert: Regionale und vergleichende Perspektiven* (Paderborn: Schöningh, 1996), 401–17.

60. Uekötter, *The Green and the Brown*, 59n.

61. Charles Closmann, "Legalizing a *Volksgemeinschaft*: Nazi Germany's Reich Nature Protection Law of 1935," Franz-Josef Brüggemeier, Mark Cioc, Thomas Zeller, eds., *How Green Were the Nazis? Nature, Environment, and Nation in the Third Reich* (Athens: Ohio University Press, 2005), 18–42; 18.

62. Staatsarchiv Würzburg Landratsamt Bad Kissingen no. 1237, Bund Naturschutz in Bayern to the Gruppenführer and Vertrauensmänner, August 28, 1935.

63. Staatsarchiv Darmstadt G 38 Eudorf no. 47, Beauftragter für Naturschutz, Gau Hessen-Nassau to the Ortsringleiter, June 4, 1938.

64. Hans Klose, "Der Weg des deutschen Naturschutzes," Klose, Herbert Ecke, eds., *Verhandlungen deutscher Landes- und Bezirks-beauftragter für Naturschutz und Landschaftspflege: Zweite Arbeits-tagung, 24.–26. Oktober 1948 Bad Schwalbach und Schlangenbad* (Egestorf: Zentralstelle für Naturschutz und Landschaftspflege, 1949), 30–46; 40.

65. Karl Asal, "Bewährung und Weiterbildung des Reichsnaturschutz-rechts," Hans Klose, Herbert Ecke, eds., *Verhandlungen deutscher Landes- und Bezirksbeauftragter für Naturschutz und Landschafts-pflege: Dritte Arbeitstagung 11. bis 13. September 1949 Boppard am Rhein* (Egestorf: Zentralstelle für Naturschutz und Landschaftspflege, 1950), 10–20; 10.

66. Westfälisches Archivamt Münster Bestand 717 file "Reichsstelle (Bundesstelle) für Naturschutz (und Landschaftspflege)," Der Direk-tor der Reichsstelle für Naturschutz, Denkblätter der Reichsstelle für Naturschutz über die künftige Wahrnehmung von Naturschutz und Landschaftspflege, June 26, 1945, p. 4.

67. Ibid., Der Direktor der Reichsstelle für Naturschutz to the Beauftragten bei den besonderen und höheren Stellen für Natur-schutz, July, 1945, p. 4. Emphasis in the original.

68. Alon Confino, "'This lovely country you will never forget': Kriegs-erinnerungen und Heimatkonzepte in der westdeutschen Nachkriegs-zeit," Habbo Knoch, ed., *Das Erbe der Provinz: Heimatkultur und Geschichtspolitik nach 1945* (Göttingen: Wallstein, 2001), 235–51.

Chapter 3

1. For an overview of the Wutach conflict, see Sandra Chaney, *Nature of the Miracle Years: Conservation in West Germany, 1945–1975* (New York: Berghahn Books, 2008), 85–113.

2. Hauptstaatsarchiv Stuttgart EA 3/102 no. 29, Regierungspräsidi-um Südbaden, Landeskulturamt to the Kultusministerium Baden-Württemberg, January 13, 1954.

3. Ibid., Schluchseewerk AG, Wozu Unterschriften zur Rettung der Wutachschlucht? (April 1954).

4. Ibid., Muß die Wutach abgeleitet werden? Wirtschaftliche Betrachtungen zum Plan der Wutachableitung durch die Schluchseewerk AG, Schriftenreihe der Arbeitsgemeinschaft "Heimatschutz Schwarzwald," issue 2, Freiburg, March 1955, p. 14. On the role of Nazi connotations in the fight over nuclear power, see Michael Schüring, "West German Protestants and the Campaign against Nuclear Technology," *Central European History* 45 (2012): 744–62; 760n.

5. Hauptstaatsarchiv Stuttgart EA 3/102 no. 29, Arbeitsgemeinschaft Heimatschutz Schwarzwald to Kultusminister Simpfendörfer, February 8, 1958.

6. Friedbert Zapf, "'Hände weg von der Wutachschlucht!'—Naturschützer boten Energiewirtschaft die Stirn," *Der Schwarzwald* 1 (2009): 4–8; 8.

7. Jens Ivo Engels, *Naturpolitik in der Bundesrepublik: Ideenwelt und politische Verhaltensstile in Naturschutz und Umweltbewegung, 1950–1980* (Paderborn: Schöningh, 2006), 164.

8. Anna-Katharina Wöbse, "Die Bomber und die Brandgans: Zur Geschichte des Kampfes um den 'Knechtsand'—Eine historische Kernzone des Nationalparks Niedersächsisches Wattenmeer," Günter Altner et al., eds., *Jahrbuch Ökologie 2008* (Munich: Beck, 2007), 188–99.

9. Ute Hasenöhrl, *Zivilgesellschaft und Protest: Eine Geschichte der Naturschutz- und Umweltbewegung in Bayern, 1945–1980* (Göttingen: Vandenhoeck & Ruprecht, 2010).

10. Landesarchiv Saarbrücken AA 320, letter of the von der Bevölkerung gewählter und bevollmächtigter Ausschuss zur Bekämpfung der Staub- und Lärmplage, February 21, 1957, p. 5.

11. Armin Simon, *Der Streit um das Schwarzwald-Uran: Die Auseinandersetzung um den Uranbergbau in Menzenschwand im Südschwarzwald 1960–1991* (Bremgarten: Donzelli-Kluckert, 2003).

12. Ulrich Linse, "Der Wandervogel," Etienne François, Hagen Schulze, eds., *Deutsche Erinnerungsorte III* (Munich: Beck, 2003), 531–48; 548.

13. Wolfgang Kraushaar, *Die Protest-Chronik, 1949–1959: Eine illustrierte Geschichte von Bewegung, Widerstand und Utopie*. Vol. 2: *1953–1956* (Hamburg: Rogner & Bernhard bei Zweitausendeins, 1996), 957, 1101.

14. Frank Uekötter, *Naturschutz im Aufbruch: Eine Geschichte des Naturschutzes in Nordrhein-Westfalen, 1945–1980* (Frankfurt: Campus, 2004), 74n.

15. Engels, *Naturpolitik*, 201.

16. Hasenöhrl, *Zivilgesellschaft*.

17. Almut Leh, *Zwischen Heimatschutz und Umweltbewegung: Die Professionalisierung des Naturschutzes in Nordrhein-Westfalen, 1945–1975* (Frankfurt: Campus, 2006), 253.

18. Hermand, *Grüne Utopien*, 118–28.

19. Wilhelm Lienenkämper, *Grüne Welt zu treuen Händen: Naturschutz und Landschaftspflege im Industriezeitalter* (Stuttgart: Franckh, 1963), 181.

20. Hauptstaatsarchiv Düsseldorf NW 260 no. 75, p. 201.

21. Hauptstaatsarchiv Stuttgart EA 3/102 no. 29, Arbeitsgemeinschaft Heimatschutz Schwarzwald to Kultusminister Simpfendörfer, February 8, 1958, p. 3.

22. Engels, *Naturpolitik*, 97–110.

23. Karsten Runge, *Entwicklungstendenzen der Landschaftsplanung: Vom frühen Naturschutz bis zur ökologisch nachhaltigen Flächennutzung* (Berlin: Springer, 1998), 87–89; Sebastian Strube, *Euer Dorf soll schöner werden: Ländlicher Wandel, staatliche Planung und Demokratisierung in der Bundesrepublik Deutschland* (Göttingen: Vandenhoeck & Ruprecht, 2013), 37–45.

24. Günther Schwab, *Der Tanz mit dem Teufel: Ein abenteuerliches Interview* (Hanover: Sponholtz, 1958).

25. Hauptstaatsarchiv Düsseldorf NW 50 no. 1215, pp. 13r, 14.

26. Uekötter, *Age of Smoke*, 174–79.

27. Terence Kehoe, *Cleaning up the Great Lakes: From Cooperation to Confrontation* (DeKalb: Northern Illinois University Press, 1997).

28. Bundesarchiv R 154/86, Sitzung des Staubausschusses der Braunkohlekraftwerke im Kölner Bezirk on August 3, 1954, p. 6.

29. Bundesarchiv B 136/5364, STBK to Bundesminister für Verkehr, July 27, 1960.

30. *Vorwärts* no. 18 (May 3, 1961), p. 20, c. 2.

31. Wolfgang Kraushaar, *Achtundsechzig: Eine Bilanz* (Berlin: Propyläen, 2008); Ingrid Gilcher-Holtey, *Die 68er Bewegung: Deutsch-*

land—Westeuropa—USA (Munich: Beck, 2001); Gerd Könen, *Das rote Jahrzehnt: Unsere kleine deutsche Kulturrevolution, 1967–1977* (Frankfurt: Fischer Taschenbuch-Verlag, 2002); Martin Klimke, Joachim Scharloth, eds., *1968: Handbuch zur Kultur- und Mediengeschichte der Studentenbewegung* (Stuttgart: Metzler, 2007).

32. Sebastian Haumann, *"Schade, daß Beton nicht brennt . . .," Planung, Partizipation und Protest in Philadelphia und Köln, 1940–1990* (Stuttgart: Steiner, 2011).

33. Anna-Katharina Wöbse, *Weltnaturschutz: Umweltdiplomatie in Völkerbund und Vereinten Nationen, 1920–1950* (Frankfurt: Campus, 2011).

34. Landesarchiv Schleswig-Holstein Abt. 301, no. 4066, Staatliche Stelle für Naturdenkmalpflege in Preussen to the Oberpräsident in Kiel, February 24, 1921.

35. Clapp, *Environmental History*, 43–55.

36. Kai F. Hünemörder, *Die Frühgeschichte der globalen Umweltkrise und die Formierung der deutschen Umweltpolitik, 1950–1973* (Stuttgart: Steiner, 2004), 165.

37. Wilhelm Liesegang, *Die Reinhaltung der Luft* (Ergebnisse der angewandten physikalischen Chemie 3, Leipzig: Akademische Verlagsgesellschaft, 1935), 1–109; 9.

38. Jens Ivo Engels, "Von der Sorge um die Tiere zur Sorge um die Umwelt: Tiersendungen als Umweltpolitik in Westdeutschland zwischen 1950 und 1980," *Archiv für Sozialgeschichte* 43 (2003): 297–323.

39. Allan M. Winkler, *Life under a Cloud: American Anxiety about the Atom* (Urbana: University of Illinois Press, 1999), 93–98.

40. Robert Lorenz, *Protest der Physiker: Die "Göttinger Erklärung" von 1957* (Bielefeld: Transcript, 2011).

41. See Hans-Peter Schwarz, *Adenauer:* Vol. 2: *Der Staatsmann, 1952–1967* (Munich: dtv, 1994), 394–401.

42. Holger Nehring, "Cold War, Apocalypse and Peaceful Atoms: Interpretations of Nuclear Energy in the British and West German Anti-Nuclear Weapons Movements, 1955–1964," *Historical Social Research* 29:3 (2004): 150–70, and Axel Schildt, "'Atomzeitalter'— Gründe und Hintergründe der Proteste gegen die atomare Bewaffnung der Bundeswehr Ende der fünfziger Jahre," *"Kampf dem Atomtod!"*

Die Protestbewegung 1957/58 in zeithistorischer und gegenwärtiger Perspektive (Munich: Dölling & Galitz, 2009), 39–56.

43. On Packard, see Nepomuk Gasteiger, *Der Konsument: Verbraucherbilder in Werbung, Konsumkritik und Verbraucherschutz, 1948–1989* (Frankfurt: Campus, 2010), 105–108, and Daniel Horowitz, *The Anxieties of Affluence: Critiques of American Consumer Culture, 1939–1979* (Amherst: University of Massachusetts Press, 2005), 108–20.

44. *Der Spiegel* no. 46 (1962): 121n.

45. Godfrey Hodgson, "Vergiften wir unsere Umwelt? Die Schäden der Schädlingsbekämpfung," *Die Zeit* no. 36 (1962).

46. *Der Spiegel* no. 46 (1962): 118.

47. This discussion of risk is greatly indebted to Ulrich Beck. For his approach, see Ulrich Beck, *Risk Society: Toward a New Modernity* (London: Sage Publications, 1992), and Beck, *Gegengifte: Die organisierte Unverantwortlichkeit* (Frankfurt: Suhrkamp, 1988).

48. *Der Spiegel* no. 19 (1964): 121.

49. David Kinkela, *DDT and the American Century: Global Health, Environmental Politics, and the Pesticide That Changed the World* (Chapel Hill: University of North Carolina Press, 2011); Linda Lear, *Rachel Carson: Witness for Nature* (Boston: Mariner Books, 2009); Rachel Carson, *Silent Spring* (Boston: Houghton Mifflin, 1962).

50. Patrick Kupper, "'Weltuntergangs-Vision aus dem Computer': Zur Geschichte der Studie 'Grenzen des Wachstums' von 1972," Frank Ueköter, Jens Hohensee, eds., *Wird Kassandra heiser? Die Geschichte falscher Ökoalarme* (Stuttgart: Steiner, 2004), 98–111.

51. For the official history of the WWF, see Alexis Schwarzenbach, *Saving the World's Wildlife: WWF—The First 50 Years* (London: Profile Books, 2011). For a muckracking history, see Wilfried Huismann, *Schwarzbuch WWF: Dunkle Geschäfte im Zeichen des Panda* (Gütersloh: Gütersloher Verlags-Haus, 2012).

52. Stephen Fox, *The American Conservation Movement: John Muir and His Legacy* (Madison: University of Wisconsin Press, 1981), 279–81, 316–22.

53. Adam W. Rome, *The Genius of Earth Day: How a 1970 Teach-in Unexpectedly Made the First Green Generation* (New York: Hill & Wang, 2013).

54. Hünemörder, *Frühgeschichte*, 267–73.

55. Indira Gandhi, *Man and His Environment* (New Delhi: Abhinav Publications, 1992), 10.

56. Thomas Robertson, *The Malthusian Moment: Global Population Growth and the Birth of American Environmentalism* (New Brunswick: Rutgers University Press, 2012); Matthew Connelly, *Fatal Misconception: The Struggle to Control World Population* (Cambridge: Belknap Press of Harvard University Press, 2008), 89n; Thomas Etzemüller, *Ein ewigwährender Untergang: Der apokalyptische Bevölkerungsdiskurs im 20. Jahrhundert* (Bielefeld: Transcript, 2007), 131, 135.

57. Klaus Gestwa, *Die Stalinschen Großbauten des Kommunismus: Sowjetische Technik- und Umweltgeschichte, 1948–1967* (Munich: Oldenbourg, 2010), 23.

58. Douglas R. Weiner, *A Little Corner of Freedom: Russian Nature Protection from Stalin to Gorbachëv* (Berkeley: University of California Press, 1999), 129.

59. Roger Cans, *Petite histoire du mouvement écolo en France* (Paris: Delachaux et Niestlé, 2006), 125.

60. Engels, *Naturpolitik*, 275.

61. Verhandlungen des Deutschen Bundestages, 6. Wahlperiode (Stenographische Berichte vol. 78, Bonn, 1971/72), 8914n.

62. For an overview, see Hans-Peter Vierhaus, *Umweltbewußtsein von oben: Zum Verfassungsgebot demokratischer Willensbildung* (Berlin: Duncker & Humblot, 1994), 110–14.

63. Hünemörder, *Frühgeschichte*, 155, 160.

64. Bayerisches Hauptstaatsarchiv MWi 28370, Der Arbeits- und Sozialminister des Landes Nordrhein-Westfalen to the Bundesminister des Innern Hans-Dietrich Genscher, April 28, 1970, p. 1.

65. Bayerisches Hauptstaatsarchiv MArb 2596/II, memorandum of May 12, 1970.

66. Monika Bergmeier, *Umweltgeschichte der Boomjahre, 1949–1973: Das Beispiel Bayern* (Münster: Waxmann, 2002). Both Max Streibl, the first incumbent, and his personal advisor Edmund Stoiber would later become prime ministers of Bavaria, mirroring a striking prominence of environmental ministries in the career paths of top politicians. As this book was going to press, the German Chancellor was

Angela Merkel, federal minister for the environment from 1994 to 1998, while Sigmar Gabriel, chairman of the largest opposition party, held the post from 2005 to 2009. Jürgen Trittin, who served for the seven years in between, was the green party whip from 2009 to 2013.

67. Deutscher Bundestag, 7. Wahlperiode, Drucksache 2802, p. 177.

68. Renate Mayntz, *Vollzugsprobleme der Umweltpolitik: Empirische Untersuchung der Implementation von Gesetzen im Bereich der Luftreinhaltung und des Gewässerschutzes* (Stuttgart: Kohlhammer, 1978).

69. Kurt Möser, "Was macht eigentlich das Geschwindigkeitslimit?" Patrick Masius, Ole Sparenberg, Jana Sprenger, eds., *Umweltgeschichte und Umweltzukunft: Zur gesellschaftlichen Relevanz einer jungen Disziplin* (Göttingen: Universitäts-Verlag, 2009), 229–39.

70. Bernd Faulenbach, *Das sozialdemokratische Jahrzehnt: Von der Reformeuphorie zur Neuen Unübersichtlichkeit. Die SPD, 1969–1982* (Bonn: Dietz, 2011), 228, 261.

71. Nepomuk Gasteiger, "Konsum und Gesellschaft: Werbung, Konsumkritik und Verbraucherschutz in der Bundesrepublik der 1960er- und 1970er-Jahre," *Zeithistorische Forschungen* 6 (2009): 35–57.

72. Karl-Hermann Flach, Werner Maihofer, Walter Scheel, *Die Freiburger Thesen der Liberalen* (Reinbek: Rowohlt, 1972), 109.

73. Gunter Hofmann, "Ein aufmüpfiger Beamter," *Die Zeit* no. 29 (July 11, 1980).

74. Engels, *Naturpolitik*, 287, 332, 334.

75. Almut Leh, Hans-Joachim Dietz, *Im Dienst der Natur: Biographisches Lese- und Handbuch zur Naturschutzgeschichte in Nordrhein-Westfalen* (Essen: Klartext, 2009), 61.

76. Hünemörder, *Frühgeschichte*, 304–29.

77. Sabine Dworog, "Luftverkehrsinfrastruktur: Zur Rolle des Staates bei der Integration eines Flughafens in seine Umwelt," *Saeculum* 58 (2007): 115–149.

78. Hasenöhrl, *Zivilgesellschaft*, 211–16; Joachim Radkau, *Aufstieg und Krise der deutschen Atomwirtschaft, 1945–1975: Verdrängte Alternativen in der Kerntechnik und der Ursprung der nuklearen Kontroverse* (Reinbek: Rowohlt, 1983), 446–50.

79. Bernd-A. Rusinek, "Wyhl," Etienne François, Hagen Schulze, eds., *Deutsche Erinnerungsorte II* (Munich: Beck, 2001), 652–66.

80. Schüring, "Protestants."

81. Holger Strohm, *Friedlich in die Katastrophe: Eine Dokumentation über Atomkraftwerke* (10th ed., Frankfurt: Zweitausendeins, 1982).

82. Klaus Traube, *Müssen wir umschalten? Von den politischen Grenzen der Technik* (Reinbek: Rowohlt, 1978).

83. Radkau, *Aufstieg*.

84. Anselm Tiggemann, *Die "Achillesferse" der Kernenergie in der Bundesrepublik Deutschland: Zur Kernenergiekontroverse und Geschichte der nuklearen Entsorgung von den Anfängen bis Gorleben, 1955 bis 1985* (Lauf an der Pegnitz: Europaforum-Verlag, 2004), 42, 663.

85. *Der Spiegel* no. 21 (1979): 20.

86. Helmut Lackner, "Von Seibersdorf bis Zwentendorf: Die 'friedliche Nutzung der Atomenergie' als Leitbild der Energiepolitik in Österreich," *Blätter für Technikgeschichte* 62 (2000): 201–26; 223n.

87. Karl Dietrich Bracher, Wolfgang Jäger, Werner Link, *Republik im Wandel, 1969–1974: Die Ära Brandt* (Geschichte der Bundesrepublik Deutschland 5.1, Stuttgart: Deutsche Verlags-Anstalt, 1986), 146.

88. Bundesministerium für Umwelt, Naturschutz und Reaktorsicherheit, *Innovationen für Umwelt und Wirtschaft: 30 Jahre Umweltinnovationsprogramm* (Berlin: Bundesministerium für Umwelt, Naturschutz & Reaktorsicherheit, 2009).

89. Hans-Dietrich Genscher, *Erinnerungen* (Berlin: Siedler, 1995), 137.

Interim Remarks

1. See Adam Rome, "'Give Earth a Chance': The Environmental Movement and the Sixties," *Journal of American History* 90 (2003): 525: "The literature on the sixties slights the environmental movement, while the work on environmentalism neglects the political, social, and cultural history of the sixties."

2. Frank Uekötter, Claas Kirchhelle, "Wie Seveso nach Deutschland kam: Umweltskandale und ökologische Debatte von 1976 bis 1986," *Archiv für Sozialgeschichte* 52 (2012): 317–34.

3. On the Sandoz fire, see Nils Freytag, "Der rote Rhein: Die Sandoz-Katastrophe vom 1. November 1986 und ihre Folgen," Themenportal Europäische Geschichte (2010), http://www.europa.clio-online.de/portals/_europa/documents/B2010/E_Freytag_Sandoz_Katastrophe_final.pdf (accessed May 21, 2013).

4. Saskia Richter, *Die Aktivistin: Das Leben der Petra Kelly* (Munich: Deutsche Verlags-Anstalt, 2010).

5. Bess, *Light-Green Society*, 72; Kevin Niebauer, "Ökologische Krise und Umweltbewegung auf der Akteursebene: Ideenwelt, Handlungsstrategie und Selbstverständnis von José A. Lutzenberger, 1968 bis 1992," Master's thesis, Freie Universität Berlin (2012).

6. See, for instance, Samuel P. Hays (in collaboration with Barbara D. Hays), *Beauty, Health, and Permanence: Environmental Politics in the United States, 1955–1985* (Cambridge, UK: Cambridge University Press, 1989), 35.

7. Ronald Inglehart, *The Silent Revolution: Changing Values and Political Styles among Western Publics* (Princeton: Princeton University Press, 1977).

8. Ronald Inglehart, Christian Welzel, *Modernization, Cultural Change, and Democracy* (Cambridge, UK: Cambridge University Press, 2005).

9. See p. 78.

10. Willibald Steinmetz, "Ungewollte Politisierung durch die Medien? Die Contergan-Affäre," Bernd Weisbrod, ed., *Die Politik der Öffentlichkeit—Die Öffentlichkeit der Politik* (Göttingen: Wallstein, 2003), 195–228.

11. Thilo Jungkind, *Risikokultur und Störfallverhalten der chemischen Industrie: Gesellschaftliche Einflüsse auf das unternehmerische Handeln von Bayer und Henkel seit der zweiten Hälfte des 20. Jahrhunderts* (Stuttgart: Steiner, 2013), 292.

12. Faulenbach, *Das sozialdemokratische Jahrzehnt*, 605.

13. See Anselm Doering-Manteuffel, Lutz Raphael, *Nach dem Boom: Perspektiven auf die Zeitgeschichte seit 1970* (Göttingen: Vandenhoeck & Ruprecht, 2008); Konrad H. Jarausch, ed., *Das Ende der Zuversicht? Die siebziger Jahre als Geschichte* (Göttingen: Vandenhoeck & Ruprecht, 2008); Thomas Raithel, Andreas Rödder, Andreas Wirsching, eds., *Auf dem Weg in eine neue Moderne? Die Bundesre-*

publik Deutschland in den siebziger und achtziger Jahren (Munich: Oldenbourg, 2009).

14. Herbert Gruhl, *Ein Planet wird geplündert: Die Schreckensbilanz unserer Politik* (Frankfurt: Fischer, 1975).

15. Kai F. Hünemörder, "Zwischen Bewegungsforschung und Historisierungsversuch. Anmerkungen zum Anti-Atomkraft-Protest aus umwelthistorischer Perspektive," Robert Kretzschmar, Clemens Rehm, Andreas Pilger, eds., *"1968" und die "Anti-Atomkraft-Bewegung der 1970er-Jahre." Überlieferungsbildung und Forschung im Dialog* (Stuttgart: Kohlhammer, 2008), 151–67; 162.

16. Wolfgang R. Krabbe, "'Rekrutendepot' oder politische Alternative? Funktion und Selbstverständnis der Partei-Jugendverbände" *Geschichte und Gesellschaft* 27 (2001): 299.

17. Kraushaar, *Achtundsechzig*, 239.

18. Susanne Schregel has described a similar phenomenon for the peace protests that immediately preceded the boom of ecology. See her *Der Atomkrieg vor der Wohnungstür: Eine Politikgeschichte der neuen Friedensbewegung in der Bundesrepublik, 1970–1985* (Frankfurt: Campus, 2011), 42–77.

19. Rüdiger Graf, "Die Grenzen des Wachstums und die Grenzen des Staates: Konservative und die ökologischen Bedrohungsszenarien der frühen 1970er Jahre," Dominik Geppert, Jens Hacke, eds., *Streit um den Staat: Intellektuelle Debatten in der Bundesrepublik, 1960–1980* (Göttingen: Vandenhoeck & Ruprecht, 2008), 207–28.

20. Tony Judt, *Postwar: A History of Europe since 1945* (New York: Penguin, 2005), 477.

21. For an overview of social movements in Germany, see Roland Roth, Dieter Rucht, eds., *Die sozialen Bewegungen in Deutschland seit 1945: Ein Handbuch* (Frankfurt: Campus, 2008).

22. In this way environmentalism also acted as a vehicle of social mobility. For instance, it is hard to conceive that Joschka Fischer, who did not have a high school diploma, could have advanced to the post of vice chancellor in any other way.

23. Eckart Conze, *Die Suche nach Sicherheit: Eine Geschichte der Bundesrepublik Deutschland von 1949 bis in die Gegenwart* (Munich: Siedler, 2009).

24. Jacob Darwin Hamblin, *Arming Mother Nature: The Birth of Catastrophic Environmentalism* (Oxford: Oxford University Press, 2013), 8.

Chapter 4

1. Hays, *Beauty, Health, and Permanence*, 491–526.

2. *Der Spiegel* no. 2 (1983): 32.

3. Jens Ivo Engels, "'Inkorporierung' und 'Normalisierung' einer Protestbewegung am Beispiel der westdeutschen Umweltproteste in den 1980er Jahren," *Mitteilungsblatt des Instituts für soziale Bewegungen* 40 (2008): 81–100; 85.

4. Deutscher Bundestag, 10. Wahlperiode, Drucksache no. 67, p. 2.

5. Kenneth Anders, Frank Uekötter, "Viel Lärm ums stille Sterben: Die Debatte über das Waldsterben in Deutschland," Uekötter, Jens Hohensee, eds., *Wird Kassandra heiser? Die Geschichte falscher Ökoalarme* (Stuttgart: Steiner, 2004), 112–38.

6. Joachim Raschke, *Die Grünen: Wie sie wurden, was sie sind* (Cologne: Bund-Verlag, 1993); and Markus Klein, Jürgen W. Falter, *Der lange Weg der Grünen. Eine Partei zwischen Protest und Regierung* (Munich: Beck, 2003).

7. The conservative alternative was founded in 1981 and ran under the name Ökologisch-Demokratische Partei (ÖDP). It continues to play a limited role in local and regional politics, particularly in Southern Germany. For more on the ÖDP, see Raphael Mankau, ed., *20 Jahre ödp: Anfänge, Gegenwart und Perspektiven ökologisch-demokratischer Politik* (Rimpar: Dolata, 1999); and Jürgen Wüst, *Konservatismus und Ökologiebewegung: Eine Untersuchung im Spannungsfeld von Partei, Bewegung und Ideologie am Beispiel der Ökologisch-Demokratischen Partei (ÖDP)* (Frankfurt: IKO, Verlag für Interkulturelle Kommunikation, 1993).

8. For the early years, see Silke Mende, *"Nicht rechts, nicht links, sondern vorn": Eine Geschichte der Gründungsgrünen* (Munich: Oldenbourg, 2011); Rudolf van Hüllen, *Ideologie und Machtkampf bei den Grünen: Untersuchungen zur programmatischen und innerorganisatorischen Entwicklung einer deutschen "Bewegungspartei"* (Bonn: Bouvier, 1990); and Josef Boyer, Helge Heidemeyer

(eds.), *Die Grünen im Bundestag: Sitzungsprotokolle und Anlagen, 1983–1987,* 2 vol. (Düsseldorf: Droste, 2008).

9. Helge May, *NABU: 100 Jahre NABU—ein historischer Abriß 1899–1999* (Bonn: n.p., n.d.).

10. See Frank Zelko, *Make It a Green Peace! The Rise of Counter-cultural Environmentalism* (Oxford: Oxford University Press, 2013).

11. Oliver Geden, *Rechte Ökologie: Umweltschutz zwischen Emanzipation und Faschismus* 2nd ed., (Berlin: Elefanten-Press, 1999), 117.

12. Frank Uekötter, *Am Ende der Gewissheiten: Die ökologische Frage im 21. Jahrhundert* (Frankfurt: Campus, 2011), 200–17.

13. See Engels, "Sorge um die Tiere"; Frank Uekötter, Amir Zelinger, "Die feinen Unterschiede: Die Tierschutzbewegung und die Gegenwart der Geschichte," Herwig Grimm, Carola Otterstedt, eds., *Das Tier an sich: Disziplinenübergreifende Perspektiven für neue Wege im wissenschaftsbasierten Tierschutz* (Göttingen: Vandenhoeck & Ruprecht, 2012), 119–34.

14. Egmont R. Koch, Fritz Vahrenholt, *Seveso ist überall. Die tödlichen Risiken der Chemie* (Cologne: Kiepenheuer & Witsch, 1978); Uekötter, Kirchhelle, "Seveso."

15. *Der Spiegel* no. 33 (1986).

16. Uekötter, *Wahrheit.*

17. Hans Jonas, *The Imperative of Responsibility: In Search of an Ethics for the Technological Age* (Chicago: University of Chicago Press, 1984).

18. Carl Amery, "Das Zeichen an der Wand," Arbeitskreis Chemische Industrie, Katalyse-Umweltgruppe Köln, ed., *Das Waldsterben: Ursachen, Folgen, Gegenmaßnahmen* 2nd ed., (Cologne: Volksblatt-Verlag, 1984), 11–13; 13.

19. Andreas Wirsching, *Abschied vom Provisorium: 1982–1990* (Geschichte der Bundesrepublik Deutschland 6, Munich: Deutsche Verlags-Anstalt, 2006), 428.

20. Publications on Chernobyl are too numerous for comprehensive annotation, but a noteworthy trend in recent years is the growing prominence of academic historians. See, for instance, Melanie Arndt, "Verunsicherung vor und nach der Katastrophe: Von der Anti-AKW-Bewegung zum Engagement für die 'Tschernobyl-Kinder,'" *Zeithistorische Forschungen* 7 (2010): 240–58; Melanie Arndt, *Tschernobyl:*

Auswirkungen des Reaktorunfalls auf die Bundesrepublik Deutsch- land und die DDR (Erfurt: Landeszentrale für politische Bildung, 2011); Karena Kalmbach, *Tschernobyl und Frankreich: Die Debatte um die Auswirkungen des Reaktorunfalls im Kontext der französi- schen Atompolitik und Elitenkultur* (Frankfurt: Lang, 2011).

21. Beck, *Risk Society*. For historians' perspectives on the concept, see Gabriele Metzler, "Demokratisierung des Risikos? Ulrich Becks 'Risikogesellschaft,'" *Zeithistorische Forschungen* 7 (2010): 323–27; and Christoph Julian Wehner, "Grenzen der Versicherbarkeit–Gren- zen der Risikogesellschaft: Atomgefahr, Sicherheitsproduktion und Versicherungsexpertise in der Bundesrepublik und den USA," *Archiv für Sozialgeschichte* 52 (2012): 581–605.

22. Gudrun Pausewang, *Die Wolke* (Ravensburg: Maier, 1987).

23. Gabriele Runge, ed., *Materialien zu Gudrun Pausewang: Die Wolke* (Ravensburger Materialien zur Unterrichtspraxis, Ravensburg: Ravensburger, 2003), 3.

24. For the official history of the Federal Ministry of the Environ- ment, see Sabine Rosenbladt, ed., *Die Umweltmacher: 20 Jahre BMU—Geschichte und Zukunft der Umweltpolitik* (Hamburg: Hoff- mann und Campe, 2006).

25. Peter Menke-Glückert, "Vorhaben der Bundesregierung zur Umweltschutz-Gesetzgebung im Hinblick auf die Energiewirtschaft," *VGB Kraftwerkstechnik* 61 (1981): 540–42; 542.

26. Wirsching, *Abschied vom Provisorium*, 377; Hans Peter Schwarz, *Helmut Kohl: Eine politische Biographie* (Munich: Deutsche Verlags- Anstalt, 2012), 390.

27. Beck, *Risk Society*, 36.

28. Bess, *Light-Green Society*.

29. Günter Wallraff, *Ganz unten* (Cologne: Kiepenheuer & Witsch, 1985).

30. Quoted after Richard Elliot Benedick, *Ozone Diplomacy: New Directions in Safeguarding the Planet* (Cambridge: Harvard Univer- sity Press, 1998), 76.

31. Benedick, *Ozone Diplomacy*, 57.

32. Bund Naturschutz archives, file "BUND Vorstand 1," minutes of the Vorstandssitzung on October 6, 1989, p. 8.

33. Spencer R. Weart, *The Discovery of Global Warming* (Cambridge: Harvard University Press, 2008). Quotation 150.

34. Jared N. Day, "Bush, George H. W.," Kathleen A. Brosnan, ed., *Encyclopedia of American Environmental History* (New York: Facts on File, 2011), 216–17.

35. Weiner, *Little Corner*, 425.

36. Carlo Jordan, "Greenway: Das osteuropäische Grüne Netzwerk, 1985–1990," *Horch und Guck* 15 (2006): 31–37.

37. Gestwa, *Die Stalinschen Großbauten*, 538.

38. Hubert Weinzierl, *Zwischen Hühnerstall und Reichstag: Erinnerungen* (Regensburg: MZ-Verlag, 2008), 195n, 198.

39. Frank Uekötter, "The End of the Cold War: A Turning Point in Environmental History?" John R. McNeill, Corinna Unger, eds., *Environmental Histories of the Cold War* (Cambridge, UK: Cambridge University Press, 2010), 343–51.

40. Institut für Umweltgeschichte und Regionalentwicklung, ed., *Umweltschutz in der DDR: Analysen und Zeitzeugenberichte*, 3 vol. (Munich: Oekom, 2007).

41. Tobias Huff, *Hinter vorgehaltener Hand...: Debatten über Wald und Umwelt in der DDR* (PhD, Freiburg University, 2012), 121, 135.

42. Andreas Dix, Rita Gudermann, "Naturschutz in der DDR: Idealisiert, ideologisiert, instrumentalisiert?" Hans-Werner Frohn, Friedemann Schmoll, eds., *Natur und Staat: Staatlicher Naturschutz in Deutschland, 1906–2006* (Bonn-Bad Godesberg: Bundesamt für Naturschutz, 2006), 535–624; 574.

43. Arvid Nelson, *Cold War Ecology: Forests, Farms, and People in the East German Landscape, 1945–1989* (New Haven: Yale University Press, 2005), 141n.

44. Rudolf Boch, Rainer Karlsch, eds., *Uranbergbau im Kalten Krieg: Die Wismut im sowjetischen Atomkomplex*, 2 vol. (Berlin: Links, 2011).

45. Nathan Stoltzfus, "Public Space and the Dynamics of Environmental Action: Green Protest in the German Democratic Republic," *Archiv für Sozialgeschichte* 43 (2003): 385–403; 395.

46. Monika Maron, *Flugasche* (Frankfurt: Fischer, 1981), 32.

47. The Socialist cause lost on the soccer field as well, defeated 2–0 by the Netherlands.

48. Rainer Hällfritzsch, Ulrike Hemberger, Margit Miosga, *Das war Bitteres aus Bitterfeld* (DVD of the Bundesstiftung zur Aufarbeitung der SED-Diktatur, 2009).

49. Michael Beleites, "Die unabhängige Umweltbewegung in der DDR," Institut für Umweltgeschichte und Regionalentwicklung, ed., *Umweltschutz in der DDR: Analysen und Zeitzeugenberichte*, vol. 3 (Munich: Oekom, 2007), 179–224.

50. Hans Dieter Knapp, "Das Nationalparkprogramm der DDR," Michael Succow, Lebrecht Jeschke, Hans Dieter Knapp, eds., *Die Krise als Chance—Naturschutz in neuer Dimension* (Neuenhagen: Findling, 2001), 35–56; 50.

51. Michael Succow, Lebrecht Jeschke, Hans Dieter Knapp, eds., *Naturschutz in Deutschland. Rückblicke—Einblicke—Ausblicke* (Berlin: Links, 2012).

52. Helge Heidemeyer, "(Grüne) Bewegung im Parlament: Der Einzug der Grünen in den Deutschen Bundestag und die Veränderungen in Partei und Parlament," *Historische Zeitschrift* 291 (2010): 71–102; 88.

53. Raschke, *Die Grünen*, 178–94, 922–24.

54. On the origins of European environmental policy, see Jan-Henrik Meyer, "Green Activism: The European Parliament's Environmental Committee promoting a European Environmental Policy in the 1970s," *Journal of European Integration History* 17 (2011): 73–85; and Jan-Henrik Meyer, "L'Européanisation de la politique environnementale dans les années 1970," *Vingtième Siècle. Revue D'Histoire* 113 (2012): 117–26.

55. Annette Elisabeth Töller, "Mythen und Methoden: Zur Messung der Europäisierung der Gesetzgebung des Deutschen Bundestages jenseits des 80-Prozent-Mythos," *Zeitschrift für Parlamentsfragen* 39 (2008): 3–17; 11.

56. Eberhard Schmidt, Sabine Spelthahn, eds., *Umweltpolitik in der Defensive: Umweltschutz trotz Wirtschaftskrise* (Frankfurt: Fischer, 1994).

57. See Dirk Maxeiner and Michael Miersch, *Öko-Optimismus* (Düsseldorf: Metropolitan-Verlag, 1996); Maxeiner and Miersch, *Die Zukunft und ihre Feinde: Wie Fortschrittspessimisten unsere Ge-*

sellschaft lähmen (Frankfurt: Eichborn, 2002); Maxeiner, *Hurra, wir retten die Welt! Wie Politik und Medien mit der Klimaforschung umspringen* (Berlin: wjs, 2007); Torsten Mann, *Rote Lügen in grünem Gewand: Der kommunistische Hintergrund der Öko-Bewegung* (Rottenburg: Kopp, 2009).

58. *Der Spiegel* no. 39 (1995).

59. I have discussed the persistence of clichés from the 1980s extensively in my *Am Ende der Gewissheiten*.

60. Roderich von Detten, "Umweltpolitik und Unsicherheit: Zum Zusammenspiel von Wissenschaft und Umweltpolitik in der Debatte um das Waldsterben der 1980er Jahre," *Archiv für Sozialgeschichte* 50 (2010): 217–69.

61. Frank Uekötter, "Die technische Katastrophe im Zeitalter ihrer elektronischen Reproduzierbarkeit, oder: Wege zu einer Historisierung der Risikotechnologien," *Werkstatt Geschichte* 63 (2013): 101–107, 105.

62. Frank Uekötter, "Fukushima and the Lessons of History: Remarks on the Past and Future of Nuclear Power," Jens Kersten et al., eds., *Europe after Fukushima: German Perspectives on the Future of Nuclear Power* (RCC Perspectives 1 [2012]: 9–31).

63. Greenpeace, ed., *Brent Spar und die Folgen: Analysen und Dokumente zur Verarbeitung eines gesellschaftlichen Konflikts* (Göttingen: Verlag Die Werkstatt, 1997), 13.

64. Anna-Katharina Wöbse, "Die Brent Spar-Kampagne: Plattform für diverse Wahrheiten," Frank Uekötter, Jens Hohensee, eds., *Wird Kassandra heiser? Die Geschichte falscher Ökoalarme* (Stuttgart: Steiner, 2004), 139–60. Quotation 152.

65. *Spiegel special* no. 11 (1995): 64.

66. Bron Taylor, ed., *Ecological Resistance Movements: The Global Emergence of Radical and Popular Environmentalism* (Albany: State University of New York Press, 1995).

67. See Manfred Görtemaker, *Die Berliner Republik: Wiedervereinigung und Neuorientierung* (Berlin: be.bra verlag, 2009); and Friedrich Sturm, *Wohin geht die SPD?* (Munich: dtv, 2009), 24.

68. There are signs that Schröder would have preferred a coalition with the Christian Democrats. See Gerd Langguth, *Kohl, Schröder, Merkel: Machtmenschen* (Munich: dtv, 2009), 206n.

69. Anthony Giddens, *The Third Way: The Renewal of Social Democracy* (Cambridge: Polity, 1998); and Giddens, ed., *The Global Third Way Debate* (Cambridge, UK: Polity, 2001).

70. Conze, *Suche nach Sicherheit*, 800–803, 808n.

71. Jürgen Hoffmann, *Die doppelte Vereinigung: Vorgeschichte, Verlauf und Auswirkungen des Zusammenschlusses von Grünen und Bündnis 90* (Opladen: Leske & Budrich, 1998), 344; Raschke, *Die Grünen*, 33.

72. Paul Hockenos, *Joschka Fischer and the Making of the Berlin Republic: An Alternative History of Postwar Germany* (Oxford: Oxford University Press, 2008), 284–88.

73. Edgar Wolfrum, *Rot-Grün an der Macht. Deutschland 1998–2005* (Munich: Beck, 2013), 217.

74. Trittin probably had little choice, as Chancellor Schröder favored corporatist negotiations with industrialists. In his memoirs, Schröder praised Trittin particularly for his loyalty and his professionalism in politics. See Gerhard Schröder, *Entscheidungen: Mein Leben in der Politik* (Berlin: Ullstein, 2007), 423.

75. *Der Spiegel* no. 32 (2003).

76. http://www.ews-schoenau.de/fileadmin/content/documents/Footer_Header/2012-03_presentation__EWS_english_.pdf (accessed May 21, 2013).

77. http://www.leopoldina.org/uploads/tx_leopublication/201207_Bioenergie_Stellungnahme_kurz_de_en_Okt2012_02.pdf (accessed August 26, 2013).

78. One could argue that the rise of a green technology sector amounts to the emergence of a fourth field of environmentalism with distinct rules and habits. However, historical research on this sector is scarce. For some insights, see Finn Arne Jørgensen, *Making a Green Machine: The Infrastructure of Beverage Container Recycling* (New Brunswick: Rutgers University Press, 2011); and Bess, *Light-Green Society*. For perspectives on the intersection between the history of technology and environmental history, see Dolly Jørgensen, Finn Arne Jørgensen, Sara Pritchard, eds., *New Natures: Joining Environmental History with Science and Technology Studies* (Pittsburgh: University of Pittsburgh Press, 2013); Martin Reuss, Stephen H. Cutcliffe, eds., *The Illusory Boundary: Environment and Technology in History* (Charlottesville: University Press of Virginia, 2010); Jeffrey K. Stine, Joel A. Tarr, "At

the Intersection of Histories: Technology and the Environment," *Technology and Culture* 39 (1998): 601–40.

79. Wolfrum, *Rot-Grün an der Macht*, 686, 707.

80. http://www.bundestag.de/dokumente/protokolle/amtlicheprotokolle/2011/ap17117.html (accessed May 21, 2013).

Chapter 5

1. Thomas Nipperdey, "Der Kölner Dom als Nationaldenkmal," Nipperdey, ed., *Nachdenken über die deutsche Geschichte* (Munich: dtv, 1990), 189–207.

2. Erich Kaiser, "Über Verwitterungserscheinungen an Bausteinen," *Neues Jahrbuch für Mineralogie, Geologie und Paläontologie* 100, 2 (1907): 42–64.

3. *Der Spiegel* no. 47 (1981): 101.

4. See p. 119.

5. http://www.handelsblatt.com/technologie/energie-umwelt/energietechnik/erster-offshorewindpark-windraeder-so-hoch-wie-der-koelner-dom/4124120.html (accessed May 21, 2013).

6. Christopher Rootes, "The Transformation of Environmental Activism: An Introduction," Rootes, ed., *Environmental Protest in Western Europe* (Oxford: Oxford University Press, 2003), 1.

7. Ted Nordhaus, Michael Shellenberger, *Break Through: Why We Can't Leave Saving the Planet to Environmentalists* (Boston: Mariner Books, 2009).

8. See Tim Jackson, *Prosperity without Growth: Economics for a Finite Planet* (London: Earthscan, 2009).

9. http://ec.europa.eu/environment/legal/law/statistics.htm (accessed May 21, 2013).

10. James David Fahn, *A Land on Fire: The Environmental Consequences of the Southeast Asian Boom* (Boulder: Westview Press, 2003), 7.

11. Mende, *Nicht rechts*.

12. Klein, Falter, *Der lange Weg der Grünen*, 105.

13. BUND, MISEREOR, eds., *Zukunftsfähiges Deutschland: Ein Beitrag zu einer global nachhaltigen Entwicklung* (Basel: Birkhäu-

ser, 2006); Bund für Umwelt und Naturschutz, Brot für die Welt and Evangelischer Entwicklungsdienst, eds., *Zukunftsfähiges Deutschland in einer globalisierten Welt: Ein Anstoß zur gesellschaftlichen Debatte* (Frankfurt: Fischer Taschenbuch-Verlag, 2008).

14. Daniel J. Fiorino, *Making Environmental Policy* (Berkeley: University of California Press, 1995), 56.

15. Elisabeth Rosenthal, "Solar Industry Learns Lesson in Spanish Sun," and Jennifer Steinhauer, "Keeping Whale off Sushi Plates Is Oscar Winners' Next Mission, " *New York Times* March 9, 2010.

Epilogue

1. J. W. Emerson et al., *2012 Environmental Performance Index and Pilot Trend Environmental Performance Index* (New Haven: Yale Center for Environmental Law and Policy, 2012).

2. epi.yale.edu/epi2012/rankings (accessed May 21, 2013).

3. epi.yale.edu/dataexplorer/countryprofiles?iso=DEU (accessed May 21, 2013).

4. Environmental Rating Agency, *G20 Report. AAA-DDD Ratings for National Environmental Performance* (Oxford: Environmental Ratings Agency, 2012). Quotations 11, 32.

5. Jan Burck, Lukas Hermwille, Laura Krings, *The Climate Change Performance Index: Results 2013* (n.l.: Germanwatch, December 2012). Quotations 14, 16.

6. Environmental Rating Agency, *G20 Report*, 11.

7. John S. Dryzek et al., *Green States and Social Movements: Environmentalism in the United States, United Kingdom, Germany, and Norway* (Oxford: Oxford University Press, 2003), 183; Chris Rose, *The Dirty Man of Europe: The Great British Pollution Scandal* (London: Simon & Schuster, 1990).

Selected Readings on German Environmentalism

Beck, Ulrich. *Risk Society: Towards a New Modernity*. London: Sage Publications, 1992.

Blackbourn, David. *The Conquest of Nature: Water, Landscape, and the Making of Germany*. New York: Norton, 2006.

Brüggemeier, Franz-Josef, Mark Cioc, and Thomas Zeller, eds. *How Green Were the Nazis? Nature, Environment, and Nation in the Third Reich*. Athens, Ohio: Ohio University Press, 2005.

BUND, MISEREOR, ed. *Zukunftsfähiges Deutschland: Ein Beitrag zu einer global nachhaltigen Entwicklung*. Basel: Birkhäuser, 2006.

Bund für Umwelt und Naturschutz, Brot für die Welt and Evangelischer Entwicklungsdienst, eds. *Zukunftsfähiges Deutschland in einer globalisierten Welt: Ein Anstoß zur gesellschaftlichen Debatte*. Frankfurt: Fischer Taschenbuch-Verlag, 2008.

Bundesamt für Naturschutz, ed. *Daten zur Natur 2012*. Münster: Bundesamt für Naturschutz, 2012.

Chaney, Sandra. *Nature of the Miracle Years: Conservation in West Germany, 1945–1975*. New York: Berghahn Books, 2008.

Dominick, Raymond H. *The Environmental Movement in Germany: Prophets and Pioneers, 1871–1971*. Bloomington: Indiana University Press, 1992.

Dryzek, John S., et al. *Green States and Social Movements: Environmentalism in the United States, United Kingdom, Germany, and Norway*. Oxford: Oxford University Press, 2003.

Engels, Jens Ivo. *Naturpolitik in der Bundesrepublik: Ideenwelt und politische Verhaltensstile in Naturschutz und Umweltbewegung 1950–1980*. Paderborn: Schöningh, 2006.

Evans, Richard J. *Death in Hamburg: Society and Politics in the Cholera Years, 1830–1910*. Oxford: Clarendon Press, 1987.

German Advisory Council on Global Change. *World in Transition: A Social Contract for Sustainability*. Berlin: WBGU, 2011.

Gissibl, Bernhard. "A Bavarian Serengeti: Space, Race and Time in the Entangled History of Nature Conservation in East Africa and Germany." In Bernhard Gissibl, Sabine Höhler, Patrick Kupper, eds., *Civilizing Nature: National Parks in Global Historical Perspective*. New York: Berghahn Books, 2012, 102–19.

Goodbody, Axel, ed. *The Culture of German Environmentalism: Anxieties, Visions, Realities*. New York: Berghahn Books, 2002.

Goodbody, Axel. *Nature, Technology and Cultural Change in Twentieth-Century German Literature: The Challenge of Ecocriticism*. Basingstoke: Palgrave Macmillan, 2007.

Hasenöhrl, Ute. *Zivilgesellschaft und Protest: Eine Geschichte der Naturschutz- und Umweltbewegung in Bayern, 1945–1980*. Göttingen: Vandenhoeck & Ruprecht, 2010.

Hockenos, Paul. *Joschka Fischer and the Making of the Berlin Republic: An Alternative History of Postwar Germany*. Oxford: Oxford University Press, 2008.

Hünemörder, Kai F. *Die Frühgeschichte der globalen Umweltkrise und die Formierung der deutschen Umweltpolitik (1950–1973)*. Stuttgart: Steiner, 2004.

Institut für Umweltgeschichte und Regionalentwicklung, ed. *Umweltschutz in der DDR: Analysen und Zeitzeugenberichte*, 3 vol. Munich: Oekom, 2007.

Kerbs, Diethart, and Jürgen Reulecke, eds. *Handbuch der deutschen Reformbewegungen, 1880–1933*. Wuppertal: Hammer, 1998.

Lekan, Thomas M. *Imagining the Nation in Nature: Landscape Preservation and German Identity, 1885–1945*. Cambridge: Harvard University Press, 2003.

Lekan, Thomas M. "'Serengeti Shall Not Die': Bernhard Grzimek, Wildlife Film, and the Making of a Tourist Landscape in East Africa." *German History* 29 (2011): 224–64.

Lekan, Thomas M., and Thomas Zeller, eds. *Germany's Nature: Cultural Landscapes and Environmental History*. New Brunswick: Rutgers University Press, 2005.

Markham, William T. *Environmental Organizations in Modern Germany: Hardy Survivors in the Twentieth Century and Beyond.* New York: Berghahn Books, 2008.

Mauch, Christof, and Kiran Klaus Patel. "Environment: Conservation versus Exploitation." In Patel, Mauch, eds., *The United States and Germany during the Twentieth Century: Competition and Convergence.* New York: Cambridge University Press, 2010, 180–93.

Mauch, Christof, Nathan Stoltzfus, and Douglas R. Weiner, eds. *Shades of Green: Environmental Activism around the Globe.* Lanham, MD: Rowman & Littlefield, 2006.

McNeill, John R., and Corinna Unger, eds. *Environmental Histories of the Cold War.* Cambridge: Cambridge University Press, 2010.

Mende, Silke. *"Nicht rechts, nicht links, sondern vorn": Eine Geschichte der Gründungsgrünen.* Munich: Oldenbourg, 2011.

Meyer, Jan-Henrik. "Green Activism: The European Parliament's Environmental Committee promoting a European Environmental Policy in the 1970s." *Journal of European Integration History* 17 (2011): 73–85.

Nelson, Arvid. *Cold War Ecology: Forests, Farms, and People in the East German Landscape, 1945–1989.* New Haven: Yale University Press, 2005.

Raschke, Joachim. *Die Grünen: Wie sie wurden, was sie sind.* Cologne: Bund-Verlag, 1993.

Radkau, Joachim. *Aufstieg und Krise der deutschen Atomwirtschaft, 1945–1975: Verdrängte Alternativen in der Kerntechnik und der Ursprung der nuklearen Kontroverse.* Reinbek: Rowohlt, 1983.

Radkau, Joachim. *The Age of Ecology.* Malden, MA: Polity, 2013.

Richter, Saskia. *Die Aktivistin: Das Leben der Petra Kelly.* Munich: Deutsche Verlags-Anstalt, 2010.

Rollins, William H. *A Greener Vision of Home: Cultural Politics and Environmental Reform in the German Heimatschutz Movement, 1904–1918.* Ann Arbor: University of Michigan Press, 1997.

Rootes, Christopher, ed. *Environmental Protest in Western Europe.* Oxford: Oxford University Press, 2003.

Roth, Roland, and Dieter Rucht, eds. *Die sozialen Bewegungen in Deutschland seit 1945: Ein Handbuch.* Frankfurt: Campus, 2008.

Schmoll, Friedemann. *Erinnerung an die Natur: Die Geschichte des Naturschutzes im deutschen Kaiserreich.* Frankfurt: Campus, 2004.

Schregel, Susanne. *Der Atomkrieg vor der Wohnungstür: Eine Politikgeschichte der neuen Friedensbewegung in der Bundesrepublik, 1970–1985.* Frankfurt: Campus, 2011.

Schreurs, Miranda A. *Environmental Politics in Japan, Germany, and the United States.* Cambridge, UK: Cambridge University Press, 2002.

Schüring, Michael. "West German Protestants and the Campaign against Nuclear Technology." *Central European History* 45 (2012): 744–62.

Succow, Michael, Lebrecht Jeschke, and Hans Dieter Knapp, eds. *Naturschutz in Deutschland: Rückblicke—Einblicke—Ausblicke.* Berlin: Links, 2012.

Staudenmaier, Peter. "Organic Farming in Nazi Germany: The Politics of Biodynamic Agriculture, 1933–1945." *Environmental History* 18 (2013): 383–411.

Stoltzfus, Nathan. "Public Space and the Dynamics of Environmental Action: Green Protest in the German Democratic Republic." *Archiv für Sozialgeschichte* 43 (2003): 385–403.

Uekötter, Frank. *The Green and the Brown: A History of Conservation in Nazi Germany.* New York: Cambridge University Press, 2006.

Uekötter, Frank. *The Age of Smoke: Environmental Policy in Germany and the United States, 1880–1970.* Pittsburgh: University of Pittsburgh Press, 2009.

Umweltbundesamt. *Data on the Environment* (CD-ROM). Dessau-Roßlau: Umweltbundesamt, 2009.

Williams, John Alexander. *Turning to Nature in Germany: Hiking, Nudism, and Conservation, 1900–1940.* Stanford: Stanford University Press, 2007.

Wolfrum, Edgar. *Rot-Grün an der Macht: Deutschland 1998–2005.* Munich: Beck, 2013.

Zeller, Thomas. *Driving Germany: The Landscape of the German Autobahn, 1930–1970.* New York: Berghahn Books, 2007.

Index